INSPIRING PROFESSIONAL WOMEN WHO

INSPIRING WOMEN PROFESSIONALS who Boss Up

Learning the ways of women on the rise making an impact.

PRESENTED BY
Women With Vision International

Copyright © 2022 by Delucslife Media

All rights reserved. This book or any portion thereof may not be reproduced or used in any manner whatsoever without the express written permission of the publisher except for the use of brief quotations in a book review.

First Printing, 2022

Book Interior Design by VMC Art & Design, LLC

ISBN: 979-8-9853309-5-3

Delucslife Media
Sheridan, WY

www.delucslife.com

Printed in USA

TABLE OF CONTENTS

Foreword by Tam Luc i

Section 1: Lifestyle 5

    Chapter 1: Before Starting, Know Why You're Doing It
with Jolisa Webb 7

    Chapter 2: Looking at Roadblocks as a Teacher
with Jasmine Jones 23

    Chapter 3: Investing in yourself with Yolanda Taylor 33

    Chapter 4: Everything is Within You to Make the
Magic with Dele Kooley 45

    Chapter 5: Don't Reinvent the Wheel, Know What
You Want and See How Everyone do it with
Christine Santori 61

    Chapter 6: Don't Let Yourself be your Own Hindrance
to your Progress and Success with Joanne Whitlock 77

    Chapter 7: Knowing your Own Definition of Success
with Wen Hsu 91

Section 2: Health **103**
   Chapter 8: Digging Deep into Your Superficial Why's
   with Dr Teisha Robertson........................ 105

   Chapter 9: Owning Our Health as a Relationship
   with Dr Deborah Howell 115

   Chapter 10: Don't Give Up Until You Find Your Purpose
   with Sue Bellion 129

   Chapter 11: Don't Give Up till the Miracle Happens
   with Karen Rubinstein........................... 137

Section 3: Business................................. **149**
   Chapter 12: Doing Things Your Way to Ignite the
   Spark Inside You with Kristen Kramer 151

   Chapter 13: Feeding Our Minds in Different Ways
   with Massiel Medina............................. 163

   Chapter 14: Taking the Leap of Calculated Faith
   with Amanda Ma 173

   Chapter 15: Creating Loyalty For Life
   with Crystal D'Cunha............................ 187

   Chapter 16: Reassess Your Definition of Success
   with Gail Meriel 205

Section 4: What's Next............................. **217**
   Stepping into the shoes of an entrepreneur by Tam Luc.... 219

FOREWORD
by Tam Luc

WHAT DOES IT TAKE TO BE INSPIRING TO OTHERS? There are so many amazing stories that I hear daily but one thing that stands out is when people are willing to do the work on themselves for personal growth and then they also consider the impact that sharing their story will have on others. We are all walking around suffering from traumas that we have dealt with in our lives. Every person is dealing with trauma in one way or the other. Sometimes the reason for getting help is our love for others, and sometimes the catalyst for getting help is hearing someone else's story of resilience. All of our healing journeys are personal, but what this group of ladies has in common, and what makes them so inspiring, is that they went through their challenges, their ups and downs, and their difficulties without giving up.

    I've been told on occasion that I am inspiring. It never occurred to me that this would happen. I did the work to get past my own pain. And these authors have done the same. The lessons you can learn from all of this is that you can be inspiring also. You don't need to have $1 million business. INSPIRATION can come from making progress by taking one step at a time. Getting 1% better every day is inspiring. So what are you going to do that will inspire another person?

There was an author in one of my books that I think about often. She was stalling the process of our interview for the book. Eventually I discovered that it was because she was scared to share a very painful experience from her past. I didn't know this, I just knew I needed to get the book done. So I reached out to her and whatever I said made her feel safe. She came onto my show, shared her truth, and took a major step toward her healing. I knew her story would help a lot of people. And it was a huge weight that was lifted off of her shoulders. A few months later we had an event where she got to share that story on stage. I didn't know she was planning to but when she did, the audience was noticeably moved. Many of them shed tears because the story was so relatable and real. Some came up to her afterward and said that they were so glad she had the courage to share because the same thing had happened to them. Later that day this author told me that she was glad we gave her the opportunity to share and that I was right. The inspiration came from getting past that pain, doing the work, and then sharing it so other people did not have to feel that pain also. I'm so proud of her and that is the reason why we continue to do the BossUp books.

So what will you do for yourself today that will inspire others tomorrow? I would love to hear about it in the next book in our BossUp series.

> You have the ability to be whatever you choose to be.
>
> —Tam Luc

SECTION 1
Lifestyle

JOLISA WEBB
Beauty in the Midst, LLC
Founder & CEO

CHAPTER 1

Before Starting, Know Why You're Doing It
with Jolisa Webb

HEY THERE, SUPERWOMEN. I AM SO EXCITED today to have my next guest. I've known her for several years, been in her presence and watched her do some amazing things. And I'm excited for her because she has now started her business. She had a lot of success in management positions, and she made a shift and now she's doing exactly what I believe she's meant to do. I'm excited to find out all the nitty gritty. I love to see when my friends are growing and doing what they really love to do.

Q: Ms. Jolisa Webb, how are you?
Jolisa Webb: I am awesome, Ms. Tam Luc. Thank you so much for having me on this forum today. I'm super excited to talk with you. Always excited to see you but definitely excited to be part of this. Thank you so much for extending me an invitation to come in and talk with you.

Q: Let's cover some of your background. First of all, you're a mom, you've gone through a divorce, you're a decorated Veteran, a retired lieutenant colonel. Now, I was in the Army, and I'm so impressed by that achievement: lieutenant colonel. You are United States Air Force, retired. Thank you so much for your service.
JW: Thank you for your service.

Q: Yes. And you are also an executive leader in the federal government. You have 35 years of executive analytical and leadership expertise in strategic human resources management and services. First of all, you don't even look old enough.
JW: Well, honey, I feel like it a lot of times, though.

Q: Tell us what you went through in the military and working in the federal government. What did you take from that experience that led you to want to start your own business?
JW: You know, Tam, I kind of backed into it to be honest with you. I was using some of my military benefits to take some classes. And our capstone project for the program was in entrepreneurship. We had to come up with a business that we wanted to do. At the time I was actually taking hospitality classes, and so I was scouring about for a

business, thinking, "Bed and breakfast? That sounds good." And I was like, "No." And then I thought, "Event planning?" because I'd been a protocol officer for many years, but then I was like, "No." And my teacher said, "Whatever it is, you should be your best client."

So, I thought about that. And I remembered when I was transitioning from the military, I met an image consultant, and their focus was on helping us transition from wearing the uniform to wearing regular clothes. So initially I was looking at image consulting. And then I saw "divorce coach" and I was like, "Whoa, wait a minute. What is that?" And when I looked into it, I said, "Yes. This is somebody that I would've loved to have when I was going through the experience of divorce."

And as I start to think about winding down from the federal government, I know I'm not ready to fully retire, so, what is something that I feel passionate about? What is something that would allow me to embrace my authenticity, allow me to expand and grow, and allow me to help others through one of the most traumatic experiences that most people may ever face? And so, I said, "Let me do this." And honestly, Tam, I would do it for free. I mean, I know that's not reasonable, but I feel so passionate about this, and I feel so much that it's my calling. My purpose in general is to help coach individuals not only when they're going through divorce, but just about relationships in general. And if there's a way to monetize that, then…

Q: It's so good. I love that you chose this because some of the things you were thinking about, event planning and image consulting and some of these other things—they all culminate in divorce coaching, which is funny because you were saying you really wanted something that had all of it. When you go through something as difficult as divorce, I've been through it, you've been through it, girl, it is a whole thing.

JW: It's an experience. We call it that. Think of it in the context of an experience. Because when you're going through divorce, it is a process. Very few people just wake up and say, "I'm gonna get a divorce." They have been thinking about it. And so that is the beginning of the process—this contemplation period where you're thinking about it and wondering whether you should stay or really get out. And so, you have that phase of it. Then you have the piece of it that most people think of, when you call the lawyers and you start with all the decisions: who gets the kids, who gets the house, who gets the cat, who gets the dog, all this stuff, all the decision-making that goes along with the divorce process itself.

Then, once you sign in ink, there's a recovery element to the experience. Because it's like, "I was planning this happily ever after, and now this is my new reality." Depending on your age or how long you've been married or whether you were the person that initiated the divorce or were totally blindsided—people can get stuck in any phase of this, to be honest with you and people often do.

In addition to working with clients, I also like to talk with other professionals like lawyers and psychologists and realtors and financial planners. Because just like you had a team when you planned your wedding, you need a team when you're going through divorce. You really do need a team. A lot of lawyers are beginning to reach out and partner with divorce coaches because they want to be able to focus on the legal stuff. They don't want to listen to all the emotional stuff. And they want clients that are credible, that are focused, that are organized. And so, working with a divorce coach like me before you even get into that process, it's normally a pretty wise investment. You might not be planning for the rest of your life, but you are planning for the immediate future, the foreseeable future. And so, you want to approach that as strategically as possible so that you can continue to be your best self moving forward.

Q: And like you said, you can get totally stuck in any of those phases. I remember I didn't want anybody to look at me for three years. I just get stuck in the feeling of "poor me." If I'd had a divorce coach during that time, especially someone who was focused on being your best self, picking yourself up, it would have been different. I remember we were talking about you as the divorce coach "confidante"—with the "e" at the end.
JW: Yes, I'm your confidante. I'm a little extra. That's what that "e" is for. It's for a little extra.

Q: I love that. And the truth of the matter is, you need to be that woman. When I think about you, Jolisa, you are a very feminine woman. You give it all and women need that power. Especially when they're going through something that's so devastating. Maybe their whole life is changing. They might have to move or they have kids and they're going through a lot of pain and difficulty. And so you need that girlfriend that is a little bit extra to say "Girl, come on now, get your butt up. Let's get this going."
JW: Yes, you do. My daughter wrote the most beautiful

song—the name of it is "Evolution of Birds"—but basically, she talks about our past life. You were fabulous in this past life, and you just forgot to fly. You were a bird at one time, this beautiful, exquisite bird and you forgot to fly. You are the bird and I'm your wings. I'm your wing through this process, which is also very fitting for me as a former Air Force person. We call each other "wingman" in the Air Force. We don't leave you behind, we never leave anyone behind.

It's very important to have a neutral person helping you, number one, because as much as your family and your friends love you and they want to support you and they want to be there for you, here's the thing about that: It can be very hard for even the best, most well-intended family member or friend to be unbiased during a period like this. Especially depending on what kind of relationship they had with the other person. Because in addition to helping you process your new normal, they are also having to think about how their relationship with this individual is going to change or not change. A lot of people forget that. So, when you have someone who is unbiased, who is neutral, it takes some of the pressure off your friends and your family so that they can just be your friends and your family, and you can have this coach who is focused solely on you, on what you want and what is your truth and helping you identify it, embrace it, and walk in it.

Q: That is so important. Let's talk about this because you've been through some ups and downs yourself. What are some lessons you've had to learn starting your business or navigating your life or career that you want to share?

JW: Well, one of the things—and this is real talk—my divorce came out of the blue, I was not expecting it. And like I told you, part of the reason this business popped up on my radar is because I was taking classes. A lot of times when you go through a divorce, there's a significant impact on your standard of living, the money. And a lot of times for women it's even more significant because we don't make as much as men to start with. So, my daughter was getting ready to go to college and I wanted to do whatever I could to minimize any impact on her lifestyle. And her dad, he did what he was supposed to do financially, so no shade on him. But at the same time, it was just my comfort zone about how we were living.

I still am employed full time with the federal government while trying to get started with this business. This is me wading in, trying to set myself up for my next step. I want to get this off the ground so that by the time I pull up stakes from the federal government, I know what I'm doing. Because nobody in my family has really done the entrepreneur thing. It's not something that I have done before and it's certainly a lot to learn—in terms of business operations, strategic communications, marketing, public relations, budgeting, and social media for someone like me who is not huge on social media.

So, it definitely challenges me. It's forcing me to move outside of my comfort zone, to figure out how to identify the resources that I don't have in order to get smarter. And the other thing about this business, in particular, is that a lot of people are not familiar with divorce coaches. It's a need but convincing people or getting people to really understand the value is tough. You have to figure out where the customers are and then how to tap into them when they're most likely to listen.

For example, I was on LinkedIn for a little while and quite frankly, even though that's where a lot of my customers really are, my target market, they won't talk about their worst on LinkedIn, honey. They don't want anybody to know they're struggling. On LinkedIn, everybody's fabulous and doing great. So how do you capture people? Knowing that social media is what it is, how do you really speak to people in a way that resonates with them and let them know they don't have to put up this facade when things are going wrong. There's somebody that can help you.

It's not always about divorcing. I can talk to you about things that may help save your marriage, too, or have conversations with you that put you in a mindset where you realize, "well, I thought I was unhappy in the marriage, but what's really going on is something totally different." Maybe it's something about you. I take a holistic approach to divorce coaching, so when I'm working with my clients, I look at it all. We come in during that first session, and we are going to have a conversation about the big picture of your life and really get grounded on where you see yourself right now. Then we'll determine what's really important to you, the most important thing for you right now.

That becomes a recurring refrain with each session because you'll discover sometimes people change and they forget to tell you that they've changed. Sometimes people change and they don't even realize that they've changed. Because we don't take time to get in touch with ourselves and sit down and reflect. So, there could be any number of things that may be going on with an individual who comes to me. But a lot of times on social media, it's "Oh, look at me. I'm so happy. My life is beautiful. I'm so great." People will talk about death. They'll talk about the death of a pet. They'll talk about the death of a parent. But nobody wants to really talk about the death of a marriage.

Q: Yes. Because it almost feels like you failed. If someone passes away, you didn't have anything to do with it. But if you lose a partner that means something you actively did or actively didn't do was the cause of it. It's very difficult for people to admit that. But one of the things I like about what you said is that sometimes you'll get the information you need, and it does not lead to divorce. It sounds to me like there's a couple things you help people with. It's the transition if they are going through a divorce, but it might be other things too. You're helping the whole woman.

JW: Yes. A large part of this is about accountability. Just like you said, a lot of people don't want to talk about it because they don't want to feel like they failed. But that's keeping you stuck, you know what I'm saying? That's a way to be disingenuous, to not be true to yourself. To me, the worst thing you can do is not be true and honest with yourself. Nobody really benefits when we're holding secrets or not being true, especially with ourselves. You may think you're doing somebody a favor. You may think you're doing yourself a favor. But it's called being inauthentic and down the road, being inauthentic is not consistent with being your best self, the highest version of yourself.

The real big reason all of this is important to me, Tam, is, well, I have a song that I listened to. I think I heard it when I was little, but for some reason the song always resonated with me. It's called "I'll Keep My Light in The Window" by Shirley Caesar. And one of the verses in the song talks about someone who's friendless and cannot find their way, so I'm gonna keep my light in my window. But for God's mercy, I would be in their place, so I'm gonna keep my light in my window. And the song says, I have been chosen for our work. I'm gonna build a better world for me and you.

And so that's a lot of the reason why I smile a lot. People are always asking why do you smile? That's my way of keeping my light on. That's my way of showing love and kindness. My coaching is another way for me to do that with people. And the reason it's important is when we're being inauthentic, when we're not being true to ourselves and who we are, it not only has implications for us, but it also has implications for other people.

Q: For everyone around you.
JW: And that's a big takeaway. When you are stuck, when you're not being true, when you're not being your best self, it's not just about you. We are all connected. And so, to the extent that you think this is just your little secret, your cross to bear, guess what? There is no shame in asking for help. I am a spiritual person. I'm a Christian person. I often tell people even Jesus buckled from the weight of the cross and had to get help. You know what I'm saying? That's real. In his human existence, that's what happened. And so, we all need a little bit of help now and then. We all do and that's what I want to do.

Q: How do you stay motivated?
JW: I have basically been teased all my life for being the person that looks at life through rose-colored glasses, wears her heart on her sleeve. I've been called an idealist, my mom said I never met a stranger. She said I was always a bubbly happy baby. I have my days, but I don't stay in them. A lot of it, I think, is just who I naturally am.

I'm very in touch with nature and just little things in

life. There are so many things that can amaze me and cause me to marvel. Just simple things. I mean, right now I am in the same position that a lot of women in America are in. I am helping an adulting daughter who just graduated from college, and I am also providing care to my 81-year-old mother who has dementia. So, I am part of the sandwich.

Q: Yes. You are sandwich generation.
JW: And then we have a 15-year-old Yorkie on top of it. So, a lot of women in this house. It gets heavy and can be a lot some days, but at the same time, what a gift to be able to help my daughter. I'm just so excited to see this person, who came through me, who is she really going to be? And then to know all the sacrifices and things that my mother did for me and to have this opportunity to help her in the sunset of her life, is priceless.

Q: It really is.
JW: We have three generations in this house. We have a total of four living, and at one point we had five. So, to be able to put things like that in context. Then I have beautiful friends, too. So, I have a great family, a great support network. Lots of beautiful friends that keep me encouraged so that even in my darkest hour, in addition to Jesus and the Lord and God, I have people that I can reach out and touch.

Q: What advice would you give to another woman who is making a transition in her life, whether it is a divorce, a new job, or a move? There's a new chapter in her life. What would you say is the first thing she should do before she starts tackling something new that she wants to do?
JW: First of all, make sure it's something you're passionate

about and make sure you understand why you're doing it. The why is what's going to sustain you when it gets hard. Because this can be hard. Well, I hate to say hard. There can be a lot of challenges or opportunities when you're starting a business. Let's say there can be a lot of opportunities.

And so, make sure you understand why you're doing this. What is driving you? That really is what's going to sustain you when you start to hit some of these roadblocks. That will keep you motivated. If you just get into something because of the money or it seems like the next big thing or people said you should, but you don't feel it in your heart, you could start heading down the wrong path very quickly. So, before you start doing anything, make sure you know why you're doing it. What about that is important to you? And what would success look like to you?

Q: So good, Jolisa. I've just been loving this conversation so much. Where can people find you? If someone is looking to get some more gems, where can they find you?
JW: You can find me at my website, www.JolisaWebb.com. And once you're on my website, you will find the links to my Facebook and my Instagram. If you want to look for those organically, I am @DivorceCoachConfidante on Instagram. You can also call me as well.

Q: Jolisa, I'm excited for all the stuff we'll be doing together. Thank you so much.
JW: I'm excited too. I'm learning so much from you, so thank you. This is just a phenomenal platform, and I'm super excited about your Women Who Boss Up initiatives. They are so powerful. I am beyond thrilled to have been selected to be part of it.

JOLISA WEBB

www.jolisawebb.com

Jolisa Webb is a divorced mother, a decorated Veteran, Lieutenant Colonel, United States Air Force, Retired, and an executive leader in the Federal government. I have 35 years of executive, analytical, and leadership expertise in strategic human resources management and services, with demonstrated success in the areas of command and control, communications, information management, personnel, training, protocol, and diversity and inclusion.

I am also CDC Certified Divorce Coach®, with a Post Baccalaureate Certificate in Health and Wellness Coaching, and the owner of Beauty in the Midst, LLC, a woman, and Veteran-owned small business coaching, and consulting company. Beauty in the Midst DBA Divorce Coach Confidante is rooted in healing presence and holistic, action- and outcome-focused philosophies.

> The worst thing you can do is not be true and honest with yourself.
>
> —Jolisa Webb

You don't have to wait until somebody gives you the opportunity. Just helping other people empower themselves, to really be in control of their life and their own future, empowers me.

—Jasmine Jones

JASMINE JONES
Beauty And The Network
Bridal Beauty Agency Owner & Business Coach

CHAPTER 2

Looking at Roadblocks as a Teacher
with Jasmine Jones

HEY THERE, SUPERWOMEN. I AM SO EXCITED today to have my next guest, Ms. Jasmine Jones, who is a brand strategist and mindset coach for beauty pros and service-based creative business owners. She's really helping them to prepare themselves for ditching the hustle-based lifestyle and having their brand be sustainable and profitable. I'm excited about this because a lot of entrepreneurs, when we first start, we just start because we have a love of the business. We have some ideas, but we never really stop to get our brand together and be really clear on what we're putting out in the world. Jasmine is a dual entrepreneur. She has a bridal hair and makeup business and a coaching business, so I'm really excited to delve into that.

Q: Jasmine Jones, how are you?
Jasmine Jones: I'm doing great. Thank you so much for having me here. I'm excited.

Q: Yes, I'm so excited to have you. So you went to beauty school. Let's start there. Why did you decide to go to beauty school? What was pushing you in that direction?
JJ: Oh, my goodness. I had not thought of going to beauty school, because I am the middle girl of three girls and my mom has no idea how to do hair. So I remember going to school sometimes and the kids would pick on me, they would make fun at me, like what kind of hairstyle is that? And I was like, you know what, I'm going to learn how to do my own hair so that I will not be made fun of. So learning how to do hair was me protecting myself.

But then it actually turned into "Oh, I actually enjoy doing this." And then by the time I was in fifth grade, my mother asked me to put some color in her hair—which is crazy, having a fifth-grader color your hair! I also remember having family members saying, "Okay, well, Jasmine's doing hair now." So by the time I got to high school, I already knew that once I graduated I'd be going right into trade school. I would learn how to do hair and then eventually start a studio. But I never did, because my idea of wanting to do cuts, colors, and all of those things, drastically shifted when I discovered bridal.

Q: What really sparked your interest in bridal beauty? I mean, bridal beauty is, like, fantasy beauty, right? It's like Cinderella's beauty. You're creating a transformation of not just the bride, but just the whole concept of the day.

JJ: Absolutely. So what triggered me to get interested in bridal? When I was in cosmetology school, I had already bought color, I had been touring studio salons, and getting all of the things. And a few months before I graduated, the girl at the front desk was like, "Hey, there's a local event, they're looking for some students to help out, and I think you would be perfect." When you do some events, you get extra credit, which helps you graduate faster, so I was like, of course I'm going to do that. So I ended up volunteering for Charleston Fashion Week, which is a five-day event. And the very last day is the bridal event. And there were probably 80 hair and makeup artists backstage doing bridal, working with models in bridal gowns. We started at like 5:00 a.m. and we didn't leave until 11 o'clock at night. It was crazy, it was intense, but I loved it!

I was like, what is this pressure? What is going on? I was just drooling in the corner, like, look at all this makeup, all these updos, and all of the amazing things that I never really knew that I wanted. So I was positioned in that room. I was offered that opportunity and that opportunity literally changed the direction of my entire life.

I ended up selling all of the things that I bought for my studio. I had hood dryers. I had some of my cosmetology teachers coming out to my yard sale buying half of the things that I bought for my studio. Bridal was calling my name, and even though that wasn't what I went to school for originally, I trusted it. And now I have a full-blown bridal hair and makeup team. Every time I follow my gut, there's always a huge benefit and reward that just feels like this is where I'm supposed to be. So that's how I got into bridal.

Q: That is so fun. That is really a production. People go all out! Women start thinking about what they want their wedding to be like when they're little girls. It's very, very cool that you figured out exactly what you wanted to do. What are some of the ups and downs you've experienced so far in your business or in your career?

JJ: When I first started my business, I was so young, I had just graduated cosmetology school. And when I went to get my first business license, I was 19 years old. So I was still a baby. But what really motivated me to get my business license is that after I graduated, I was like, "I'm definitely going to try out this bridal thing." So I was applying for different jobs, to get a position where I could learn and assist and join a well-known salon in my area. I am from Charleston, South Carolina. So if anybody knows about Charleston, it's very fancy, it's very Southern belle, and some of the salons that I was applying to were predominantly Caucasian salons. I had an amazing résumé. Not to toot my own horn, but people would see my résumé and they would say, "When can you start? What is your availability?" And I would have the job over the phone, my voice is kind of peppy and kind of bubbly.

But I guess they thought that I looked like something else. So when I actually showed up to tour the salon, I would go there and the receptionist would look like, "Oh, my gosh, is she here to get her hair done? We don't really know how to do her hair texture." And then they would just be like, "Oh, you're Jasmine." And I'm like, "Yes, that was me on the phone." And from having the job over the phone, when can you start, what's your availability, it always turned into, "We just want to make sure that whoever gets to be a part of our team, that they're a right fit and that they blend with our current stylists." They didn't have any African-American stylists on their team or they would be like, "Oh, you can be the relaxer girl." And I'm like, "I'm more than a relaxer girl!" So I just got tired of being overqualified but being disqualified because of my skin color.

I am very resilient and even though those doors got closed in my face, I thought, "How can I make my own door? How can I lift my own opportunity?" So that's what really led me to starting my own business. And some things that I really had to kind of get over are that I was young and I had a lot of mindset blocks. Most of the rooms where I went to network, nobody looked like me. Nobody looked like me, nobody was 19 or 20, everybody had been in the industry for years, and I'm new with my little bridal company and I just remembered feeling so out of place. People would look over me. They would think that I worked at the event or that I wasn't there networking for my own business. It's like, "Oh, what business are you here representing?" And I'm like, "I'm here doing my own business." And it's like, "Oh, that's so cute." And I'm like, "No. I'm a force. This is not adorable."

So that was just something that I really had to personally overcome. I had to be bold and confident in what I was there to do and release any kind of self-judgment that I had going on, making me think that I wasn't qualified to be in those rooms or that, "Who am I kidding? This isn't something that a little brown girl could do in this location," because at that time I didn't see any bridal companies that were Black-owned.

So I had to create my own lane. And that was the biggest thing that really helped me. I started showing up as my true self. I stopped trying to look like, sound like, talk like, be like everyone else. And that is truly when my business started to skyrocket. It took me a couple of years to really stand confidently in who I was as a person and stop trying to mimic or blend it in so much and really be confident standing out.

Q: Yes. That is very good. I can relate on so many levels to that story, you know, trying to figure out how you can get in the room, and being overlooked. It's something that a lot of us women of color have to go through, Black females especially. So what has kept you motivated?

JJ: A couple of things have kept me motivated. One, I always go back to why I started. Once my business started to really grow, I started to get a lot of people asking me, "Hey, how are you doing this? What is social media? How do I network? How do I build my business? How do I grow teams?" And what really has motivated me is that while I know that I'm helping myself, I also know that I'm helping future generations to come. And I'm actually helping to empower people by teaching them how to financially empower themselves and create money on their own and not always having to look to somebody else.

If you want to get paid today, get paid today. You don't have to wait until somebody gives you the opportunity. Yes, you can make money today. So really just helping other people empower themselves with the education and information to set themselves up, to really be in control of their life and their own future. That's what keeps me motivated. And knowing that I'm operating in my truest purpose. For a lot of people who used to work in the hustle, we gravitate to who's going to make the most money so I can pay my rent, pay my bills? But sometimes those don't necessarily light you up and make you happy. And the pathway that I'm in right now, everything I'm doing gets me so excited. I just got off a call with one of my clients and it gave me so much energy, so much joy, and it just reminded me that this is why I'm doing what I'm doing. This is why it's important. It's not just about me. My purpose is tied to so many other people, whether they just hear a word of inspiration from me or I show them how to do social media or create a business system or whatever it is. That's what really keeps me going.

Q: So good. You almost answered the next question, but I'm still going to ask it. What advice would you give another woman in a situation where she has had some roadblocks, some difficulties, she's really wanting to get herself going, start her own business. She wants to follow her dreams. How does she do it? How should she start?

JJ: One thing I like to tell people is I don't give sugar-coated advice. And I think that's why people like me. So roadblocks are going to come; roadblocks are always going to come. And for me the biggest piece of advice, because I can get very emotionally attached to some of my feelings, forgetting that my feelings are just temporary and I can always move through them. So I would say that anytime you get a roadblock, look at it and ask, "What is this teaching me?"

And check in to see if there's something that's personally stopping you. For me, I had a lot of self-doubt. A lot of, "I don't know if this is for me," a lot of imposter syndrome. And so I always have to go back to the root cause of that thought and reframe it. Why *not* me? Why am I not qualified for this? Why don't I feel confident enough? What do I have to do to gain that confidence?

And most of the time you'll gain a lot of clarity on some of these doubts just by taking action. For me, if I never felt like "this is the room that I need to be in," I wouldn't have taken the action to actually show up and keep going to those events. And going to those events, it really made me realize, "Okay, like I *am* qualified for this, I *can* be in these rooms." Those are some of the things that really helped me. Challenging my thoughts. I will be honest: I used to be a person who didn't focus on mindset. I just wanted the strategy. I'm like, "Let me just get the strategy, let me just learn how to go and accomplish X, Y, Z, and the mindset work can help me later." I thought I didn't need the mindset to work, right?

But my mindset now has really helped me navigate any other situation that tries to present itself as a roadblock. I'm just like, "You know what? I already dealt with this." Maybe it was last year or two years ago, and the situation was a little bit different. But how did I overcome that block and how can I actually utilize that to make this current roadblock tiny, because I've already dealt with it? So learning how to deal with it is going to help you so much with anything that comes along as you continue your journey.

Q: As you continue your journey. Yes, very true. I know people are going to be like, "I want to find Jasmine, I want to know everything she's doing. Where are you on social media and what is your website?
JJ: So you can find me on social media at BeautyandtheNetwork if you want to get glammed up for your wedding if you're in the Carolinas or Tennessee or

Georgia. And if you go to the link in my bio on Instagram or on Facebook, you'll be able to go to the coaching side of my website, which is www.alter-image.com/bized. So that's where you can find all of my educational information and links to my podcast and all of the fun ways that you could work with me if you're ready to get out of hustle mode and create a business that you really enjoy.

Q: It's been such a joy talking to you today, and I'm really excited to see how you're going to grow your business. Thank you, Jasmine, for being here.
JJ: Thank you. Thank you so much for having me.

JASMINE JONES
www.alter-image.com/bized

Jasmine Jones is a Brand Strategist & Mindset Coach for Beauty Pros & Service Based Creative Business Owners who're ready to ditch the hustle based lifestyle & build a brand that's profitable & sustainable with less effort. Jasmine is a Charleston, Sc Native who received her cosmetology license after attending beauty school right after graduating high school

After One year out of Beauty school Jasmine ended up starting her Bridal Beauty Business at the age of 19 after facing job diversity challenges. She is an advocate of creating your own lane, pricing yourself at a premium, and integrating your authentic personality into your marketing to have an impactful and purpose driven business.

She now coaches beauty professionals and creative service based business owners the proper backend systems they need to automate their business so they enjoy more of what makes them happy vs a business that runs their life.

YOLANDA TAYLOR
At The Style Table
CEO

CHAPTER 3

Investing in yourself
with Yolanda Taylor

HEY THERE, SUPERWOMEN. I AM SO EXCITED today to have my next guest. One reason I'm so excited is that I've known this woman for most of my life. I knew her back when we lived in the same neighborhood in Cincinnati, Ohio. I met her when my mom was doing her and her sister's hair. We went to the same high school. We became friends as young women. I think we got reconnected when we were in our twenties and it's amazing that we've stayed friends for many, many years. We both became flight attendants. She's very much a part of my life journey. She was there for most of the major events in my life, and I'm excited because this is a new chapter for her and I have always known her to be this person. Ms. Yolanda Taylor, an amazing wardrobe stylist, has actually been doing this for many, many years. She wasn't getting paid for it, but she has many, many years of experience styling me, styling all of our friends.

Q: So Yo, how are you?
Yolanda Taylor: I am fantastic. I'm so excited to be here. Thank you for having me.

Q: We go way back. I've always known you to be that person. I used to tease you all the time, like, who gets on the treadmill and watches fashion shows? Who does that? Well, you do that. And you had 31 years as a flight attendant, traveling all over the world, looking at fashion all over the world. You've been to Milan, you've been to France, and that's just the beginning. Being a flight attendant does make you more open to culture and what's available to you. And finally you took that leap, that bossing up journey into the fashion industry. So let's start with that interest in fashion. Where did that come from?
YT: I would say from the moment that puberty set in and I looked down and I had boobs and I was an awkward teen. I had, like, these big feet and I was tall. I knew I couldn't play sports because I was so uncoordinated, but I did see a fashion magazine—remember Forest Park High School? In the library there was an *Ebony* magazine, and in the back of the magazine, it was a fall edition, was the Fashion Fair section. I saw all these tall, beautiful women, and I was fixated on this woman with a yellow, one-shoulder dress that you could wear right now and be fabulous. That was back in I would say 1982. But I mean, you could put that dress on right now and look fantastic, for real. It was so gorgeous. Then from

there I just was obsessed. Absolutely obsessed. Every little penny I got from allowance, Christmas money, my little jobs, I spent every penny on some kind of clothing item.

Q: It's funny because you're similar to my mother, whereas I was never that girl. My mother was that woman who had the jewelry and the clothing and would freshen up her lipstick, you know, she was just from that era. And I depended on her a lot as I was growing up. She loved to shop and she would always have something. Now you've become that person who's always like, okay, put this lipstick on, put this necklace on. I really appreciate that because, when you are a public person, when you're speaking and you're out there getting out of your own shell, putting your business out there, you need people like this. You need people that are going to help you show up as your best self. What are some of the ups and downs or hurdles that you've had to go through, whether in life or as you were starting or growing your business?

YT: I created the name At the Style Table in 2013, because I said, "Okay, I'm gonna do it," because as I started to come closer to retirement, I was really ready. But I was too afraid to take that leap. I also had the crutch of having a job as a flight attendant. So I did everything in baby steps. I bought the website name, the domain name. I started writing some blogs and collecting things. But I never really put the pedal to the metal. After a while I just said, "I've got to do this. I love doing this." I was doing personal shopping, makeovers and wardrobe edits for friends, family, acquaintances and even a political candidate . I'm shopping for myself. And then finally you just were in my ear, like, "You should just do this. This is what you do."

I do it because it's about going after my dreams, legacy and goals during the second half of my life. I want to be of service to women to help them reach higher levels of personal, career or business success.

Q: I love that you brought that up, because that is a common thing. And you have learned to shift your mindset. A lot of people do feel like it's a failure rather than seeing it as just one of the things that you had to go through to learn a little bit more about what you're doing. And I'm really proud of you because you have come quite a long way. You walked away from a 31-year job, and started doing what you really love to do. What is motivating you the most right now, do you think?

YT: A couple of things I would say—time and legacy. What I'm leaving to my grandchildren. I have three granddaughters. So I want to be a part of the solution for women and that's what is motivating me. And of course, money.

Q: I think it's amazing because what you do is so needed. I don't know how many times I've just stood there thinking, "I don't have anything to wear." That is a very scary feeling. I don't like to figure out my wardrobe, I put it off, and I think a lot of women are like that. They've done all the other things, but now you've got to stand in front of the crowd and deliver. You have to look a certain way or you will not get the respect. All your work will be just down the drain if you don't show up. And that's part of showing up. Earlier you were talking about fashion as part of a woman's self-care. Tell me more about how you see this as a part of your self-care.

YT: As my business is evolving, as I'm bossing up, I'm

putting together the things I know best. I feel like I know fashion. I know how to dress a woman. I'm over 50. So when women reach age 40, that's often when our bodies start changing. So, I know you. I understand you. I know what you're going through.

It's a struggle to look in the closet. You're taking care of kids. You're taking care of your husband. You're running a business. You are busy and things come up all of a sudden. Guess what? An opportunity has come up. I've got to go speak. I've got an opportunity to do a book cover. I've got all of this coming up and I don't have any time. And nothing's more demoralizing than to go into the closet and go, "I have nothing to wear." Or the thing that you thought you could wear is a little too tight. It's uncomfortable. And so it's depressing. Now you have to find something else. That's stress. That's extra stress that I want to help remove from your life. So I want to be a part of your self-care. It's like when I need to go get my hair done. I can't do my hair myself. I need to go in, have somebody do it, and keep it moving.

Q: It's so true. What would you tell a woman who has maybe been in a very comfortable situation, a job they've been doing for a long time, or in the case of some of our female friends, they're empty-nesters, and they're wanting to make a change in their life? They want to start something that maybe they've had a passion about. What would you encourage them to do first?

YT: First, look at what you love to do. Because if you're making a change from something that's safe, you have to really be passionate about the next thing, otherwise it's gonna be terrifying and you're not going to finish it. You're not going to make that leap. It won't be worth it to make that leap if you're not passionate about what you do and what you want to do.

Q: How does it feel as a person who's starting something new when you don't know all the answers? Did you feel like you had to know everything before you started?
YT: Yes. I totally get it because I was one of those people that felt like I had to do everything and it all had to be ready. All that does is hold you back. Because during this process, what I've learned—and I say this over and over in my head—I've learned to not let the perfect get in the way of my progress. I've even had other business owners who have reminded me, "Don't worry sis. Don't let the perfect get in the way of your progress." So I say that to myself all the time. Anytime I feel stressed, that's what I say to myself and remind myself.

Q: That's awesome. Who would you say is your ideal client? The woman that you just love working with.
YT: You.

Q: Yeah, because I'm the one who needs it! Like, literally, I am the person.
YT: Well, it's a woman who is in my age group. It's easy because I'm you. I'm my own avatar. If I didn't love it so much, I would definitely hire someone because I'm busy. I don't have time. You just don't have a whole lot of time to think about it. That's the last thing you want to think about. You just want to get dressed, look good, and get out the door and make that impact.

Q: Another thing we were talking about is the impression you make. I know I've been guilty of this. We sometimes dismiss the importance of the way we look, but it's so important—the impression that you make when you've been doing your hard work. Any woman that has to make an impression, whether she is a business owner, speaker, politician, anyone. If you have to go out into the world and get someone to listen to you, you have to look a certain way, fortunately or unfortunately.

YT: You do. For women, it kind of stinks. A guy can show up in a polo and khakis and get the job done, or a shirt and a tie, and they just walk in. But for women, there's always that extra scrutiny for us. There are fewer female speakers. So for female speakers, you're really being judged because you're the minority, being a woman. But it's everybody—women judge each other. Oh, look, why does she have that on? You have all of that. Especially when you're on stage delivering the information, you have to feel like you look good in those clothes. You don't want to be up there like, "Oh, my God, is this sticking out?" or "Is that hanging out? No one's clapping. No one's excited. Did I wear the wrong color?" There's so much we're thinking.

Q: Girl, I just had a meeting recently and I had looked at everything I wear. What I had on was good, but still in the back of my mind, I was thinking, "Oh, is my bra showing? Is this bulge hanging out?" You're thinking a lot, so if you have someone who has put your stuff together, then you know it looks good. You don't get so distracted by all those conversations in your head.

YT: Right. Because think about it. That could be taking 10 percent of the information from your mind that you could be delivering effectively, because you're worried about something having to do with your clothes. But, yeah, as women, we're always being judged by everybody. So it matters.

Q: It does matter. Both of us are tall, so I know one of the things you specialize in is tall women. You have had that interest for at least 20 years. I've heard you talk about the tall-woman industry for years and the need there. It's still a need. You wouldn't think that would be the case. But how do you help someone who is tall?
YT: Well, first off because I'm tall and I have a 33-inch inseam and really long arms, I totally get it. It's largely knowing the designers. I know the designers, I know the stores that will have good-quality items. Unfortunately what happens is, you'll find something in a stall, but then the stall is sold out because there's just not enough.

Q: That's right.
YT: That is the number-one problem. When you go to buy something, there's just not enough. And there are very few stores that specialize in tall women's clothing. If you are a plus-size woman and you're plus-size and tall, there are more options. I mean, surprisingly, there are more options for you than someone who's between a four and a 16. A size 14 or 16 is the average American woman, so those clothes are tougher to find. It's tougher to get those things because once they hit the stores, they're gone.

Q: So what would you say to a woman who wants to start her business, but she might be a little scared. What would be your advice for her?
YT: To save money and save time, it sounds crazy, but hire

a coach. Hire a coach so you have a roadmap. I'm a big believer in coaches and because what you don't pay on the front you're gonna pay on the back. I always say that; my mom always said that.

So go ahead and invest in yourself and get a coach and get a roadmap. Because then it doesn't seem so scary and you're less likely to be flailing around trying this and throwing everything against the wall to see what sticks. I wish I would've had a coach when I tried to start my tall women clothing line. That was back when I had my big Dell computer and I was researching the online shopping industry. Back then, like 2003, it was like they were expecting 50 percent of the shopping to come from online. But even with that, there's still not enough clothes for tall women that are good quality.

Q: I am just so proud that you finally got going. Where can people find you if they're interested in working with you, if they need a wardrobe stylist or if they have questions about any of the things they've heard? Where could they reach out to you?
YT: You can reach out to me @AtTheStyleTable on LinkedIn, Instagram, and Facebook. I am At The Style Table LLC, and you can also see videos by At the Style Table on YouTube. Please subscribe to my channel!

Q: I love that.
YT: We talk about women's style issues and how they've made that transition and how they're going through all those things. Please hit me up on www.AtTheStyleTable.com as well and let's talk. Let's talk about your style dilemmas and help you get you ready for everything that you need. I'm a one-stop shop.

Q: I love it. Oh, my goodness, I'm so glad that we got a chance to talk and I am also looking forward to all the things that we are planning to do this year.

YT: Let me add one more thing. For you ladies who are looking for a stylist, remember, don't wait to lose weight. You can't wait. That opportunity's coming right now. The opportunity's not waiting for you to lose that last 10 pounds. Hire a wardrobe stylist. We'll take care of all of that for you.

Q: I am so glad you said that! You're gonna hold up your whole life procrastinating on that. You can look beautiful at any size, as long as you have someone who knows how to style your body type and knows how to help you out. Yolanda, I look forward to talking to you more.

YT: All right. Thank you for this opportunity.

YOLANDA TAYLOR

Yolanda Taylor (Yo Taylor), CEO and Founder of, At The Style Table LLC, is a wardrobe strategist, consultant, lifestyle and living blogger, and host of At The Style Table Show. She discusses the style challenges facing women. She offers styling services and strategies to help women align their style with their current and future lifestyles. She works with busy professionals, entrepreneurs, and everyday women who want to update and or transition their style through the aging process. Inspiring and supporting women is her daily mission.

> Don't let the perfect get in the way of your progress.
>
> —Yolanda Taylor

DELE KOOLEY
Dele Kooley Coaching
Founder, CEO

CHAPTER 4

Everything is Within You to Make the Magic
with Dele Kooley

HEY THERE, SUPERWOMEN. I AM SO EXCITED TO have my next guest. She's like a sister from another mister. I'm excited because she has started her coaching business and you'll see that really her whole life has been in the making for just what she's doing right now. She has a diverse background that includes 20 years as an Air Force family member and Department of Defense civilian working at three law enforcement agencies as well as navigating corporate America. And she's bringing all that to her amazing life coaching business. I'm so excited to have her here.

Q: Dele Kooley, how are you
Dele Kooley: I am fantastic, Tam. Great to see you.

Q: You have experience in human resources, training, program and project management, financial management, culture development, and diversity and inclusion. Now you're starting to channel your background into helping people navigate their careers and lives—they fit together, of course, because figuring out your career means figuring out the lifestyle you want. But let's start at the beginning. Why did you decide to go into coaching?
DK: Oh, I was born to be a coach. I always say my mom put me in my first leadership and development program when I was seven years old. There's always been this leadership and development component to every part of my life. In every job I've ever had, I've somehow found a way to be allowed to take on an additional duty around coaching or facilitating. It's just been an evolution over time and a calling that's just gotten louder and louder and louder to the point where it can't be ignored.

Q: It's interesting because you really are a successful businesswoman. You have a great career, you work for an amazing company, you're doing a lot of great things at your company, working in the diversity, equity, and inclusion space. Why the calling to go into entrepreneurship?
DK: Yes, I work at an amazing company with a fantastic culture and just amazing people. I have hit the jackpot when it comes to work and all of the things that I get to do

every day. Even in my current climate, I find myself coaching other leaders, coaching my team, having people come to me and ask me for coaching. There's no shortage! People just find me. I don't have to ask for clients. I got to a point where I was turning people away and trying to consider, how am I going to be able to actually provide service to this many people? And right now, more than ever, life coaching is an investment in your mental health.

Q: Oh, totally. I think we need to start paying more attention to our mental health and more attention to what we want in our life. In past generations, and even in my generation, there have always been things steering us one way or the other. But I think COVID made us actually start realizing we can make major decisions, major life changes, and we need to ask ourselves, "Do I really want this in my life? What do I want my life to look like?" So I think you're exactly right. What are some of the ups and downs that you've had to go through, whether in starting a new business in your life in general?

DK: Oh, that's a loaded question. I spent 20 years as a military family member, following my ex-husband around to get him to the top 3 percent of the Air Force. Supporting him in his role as a leader. And I loved every moment of it. I spent 20 years married and started raising two bonus children before I had one of my own, being invested in their lives, and then having three children of my own.

Then on the eve of my 36th birthday, I found out my marriage was going to be coming to an end. I had spent my entire life focused on raising children, being the secondary income in a family, and giving up career after career after career. Because that's what the military asked of us in order to live around the world. I had to give up my job. When I moved from Arizona to Italy, there were no jobs in Italy that I could take. I gave up all of these careers, and then I found out that my marriage is coming to an end.

I would definitely say, personally, that was the pivot point that changed my life. That is when my entire life had ceased to exist. And now I had to come up with a new plan. I had spent 20 years pivoting—pivot to an emergency communications specialist, pivot to a stay-at-home mom, pivot to Jack of all trades, a person who leads outdoor excursions, girl scout troop leader, and art teacher. Every move was a pivot.

I'd spent my entire life pivoting and now here I was with the carpet having been yanked out from underneath my feet. And that wasn't all, because then I had a major health scare as well. And so now I'm getting treatment to address my health issues, my marriage is coming to an end, and I have no idea what I'm going to do. I made $18,000 a year as a furloughed civilian, and I was the secondary income, so I was not even sure I could take care of my family. Because I'd never had to. I had just taken care of kids—I mean, taking care of all the things except for making the money.

Q: Yes. You're in a different country and you have to make real decisions. Like, what do I do? Where am I going to go? How can I take care of us? Oh, man.
DK: I could see that no matter what option I took, I would only be able to stay halfway through my oldest daughter's senior year of high school. Which meant she would be halfway through her senior year, going through a divorce, and moving to a new country and new school. That just

didn't feel fair to me. It didn't feel fair to put her through that. So I made a decision.

I literally was laying in my bed one weekend, and it was like a bolt of lightning shot through the top of my head. I sat straight up in bed and I said, I'm leaving. I was catapulted out of my bed, down the stairs, and I said to my ex-husband, "I'm leaving. I'm taking the kids and I'm going back to the U.S."

Now, there were a lot of things that had to happen for me to actually do that, and I left with $1,500, four suitcases, and a girl. And I got two tickets, they were $17 a piece, and I flew on a C17—a giant airplane that takes cargo. It's not a passenger plane. And the $17 covered two peanut butter and jelly sandwiches, a can of soda, a bag of chips, and a bottle of water. That was the flight meal that they gave you in a box with a plastic knife so you could spread your own peanut butter.

So you asked what the big challenges were. The big challenge was first, "What do I do?" I've never had to make a decision like this, and this is a life-altering decision. Because it's not like I can just keep my job and keep doing what I'm doing and just change houses. I literally had to change countries and find a job and a place to stay. I called my best friend and said, "I know that we talked about this, but I have just hit the eject button and I am in free fall. I am coming in hot. Can I please stay with you while I figure out what I'm going to do? Can Sydney—my daughter—can she stay with you until I figure it out? Can I put her in school?"

She and I had met two moves before that, when we were both stationed in Mountain Home, Idaho, together. And so, thankfully, she and her new husband came and picked us up from Joint Base Lewis McChord, and it was a Friday afternoon, school started on Monday. So we missed the enrollment. And on Monday morning, I took my daughter—in true Air Force fashion, her entire life was us throwing her into things with little to no preparation, other than what we shared with her as we were driving her to wherever we were taking her, whether it was an Italian ballet school or a swim school. I took her on a Monday and enrolled her in school, drove her into downtown Seattle after school, dropped her off at a boathouse, and said, here's your new sport and school starts tomorrow. And I'm going to go look for a job.

I had a job interview. I had gone through several interviews on the phone, and I just knew that this was going to be the job. I knew it was going to be the job. Unfortunately, like so many people in the military who are transitioning, I found that this leader, who was a Microsoft millionaire, Microsoft had purchased his company, and he didn't understand what my resume meant. He was actually a little bit rude about it. And he was like, "What does this mean? How do I know that this letter from a two-star general means anything? Can anybody get one of these?" And I was just taken aback. Because that general only wrote three letters a year and that man wrote a letter of recommendation for me. Not only did I have his letter of recommendation, I had two colonels as well. And if you have a military background, you know that's a big deal.

But this man was kind of like, "So what?" Needless to say, I didn't get the job. But everything works out as it should because it was the best thing that ever happened. By the way, the person he *did* hire, her resume ended up on my desk when I was a hiring manager several years down the road. So it really did work out exactly the way it should have, but at the time, it was devastating. Because that was the only egg I had in my basket.

Q: What allowed you to do that though, Dele? How many women have found themselves at a very difficult crossroads in life and been unable to take action? You sat up in bed and you said, "I'm leaving." What allowed you to decide that?

DK: That was divine intervention. At that moment, I literally felt like I had had a lightning bolt shoot through the top of my head. And yes, my gosh, I can't tell you how many times I questioned my ability to take care of my children on my own. Would I be able to find a job? Would I be able to find daycare for my children? All of those things had kept me in a place of being stuck. If I'm being totally honest, I was scared and I was stuck for a really long time.

Then I took action, and I took a risk. I had been at a wedding with this friend that picked me up. I had been out there the year before for my son's high-school graduation and for her wedding. While I was at the wedding, I met a Technical Fellow at Microsoft, who was the groom's mentor. I sat next to him at a table that I was not assigned to. I swapped tables because I met someone that I really enjoyed, so truly divine intervention. Because had I not sat at the wrong table, and had I not sat next to this man, he would not have said to me, I'd like to offer you a job.

I was going back to Germany, but the point is that having that conversation with him taught me two things. One is to always have a resume that's ready to go. So, every year, I meet with my resume writer, and I update my resume. I take an inventory of what I've done over the past year. What do I want to do next year, and I write my resume for the job that I want in the future. If there's a skill, I need but don't have for the job I want, I figure out how to get that skill and I go get it. Always, always, always have an up-to-date resume. Don't wait until you're looking for a job.

Second, had I not been open to thinking about my life differently, I never would've had the courage to do it. Because, in my mind, I was going to be married forever, and I was going to work for the Department of Defense until the day that I retired, and that was going to be my life. That was it. But because God saw fit to move me next door to this woman in Mountain Home, Idaho, we became friends. All of these things had to happen in order for me to get to the point where I hit the eject button with no parachute and said, I'm coming in hot.

Q: Coming in hot and ready to make a change. And one other thing is that you seem to possess confidence in yourself and your ability to make things happen. It may be because of your background and having to go through so many changes and having to pivot so often just growing up. What keeps you motivated now?
DK: My children. Being really clear on my why and what is my anchor—not as in the anchor that weighs me down, but the anchor that keeps me centered. You can't hit the eject button and leave two of your children behind without knowing that you're going to figure it out. Failure is not an option. And when I say failure's not an option, a lot of people are like, failure's good, you learn. Yes. That is a failure with a lowercase F. What I'm talking about is a failure, all caps, with exclamation marks! Meaning, you're giving up. As the master of the pivot, it didn't matter what was happening in my life, failure was not a choice.

That's where the confidence comes from. I know that no matter what happens, I'm not going to allow my children to go homeless. I'm not going to allow them to not be able to have the basic necessities. When I left with $1,500, four suitcases, and a girl, I knew that I would figure something out. My first step was to recognize—and this is something I share with my clients—mindset is everything. The thoughts that you have will create your results. For me, the thought that I had was, "Failure's not an option. I'm going to figure this out." I took the first step. I arrived in the U.S. Now what? Okay, call your friend. That's the only person you know.

By the grace of God, my friend answered the phone and then was willing to pick me up from the airport. And we stayed with her. I went to the job interview. I didn't get the job. Within days of that, I was on the floor sobbing because I had just made the biggest mistake of my life. I remember my girlfriend's husband came home and he was like, we need to talk. He reminded me that I wasn't alone. It's true, you're never alone. Whether it's the one person that you know or all of the people that you know. Because even today, I believe in the power of who, not how. And who, not how simply means that we get stuck because we don't know how to do something. I had no idea how I was going to pull this off. No idea. I had to ask for help. I had to be willing to. And as a woman, in particular, I had to get comfortable with accepting help from people, and I was not comfortable with that. So the first thing was getting comfortable with accepting grace from others, accepting help, and asking for help. That's another thing I talk to my clients about. If you've ever watched Batman, you know they shine that big bat signal when Batman is needed, and

Batman knows that he's supposed to come. If you don't tell people what you need, they can't help you. They cannot help you. Because no one—we are all humans, that's all we can be, that's all we were created to be—no one can read minds. The only way that they will know what you need is if you tell them.

So I borrowed money from my parents and I went back and got my two children. When I came back all three of my children slept in one room together, and I slept in another room at my friend's house. I had work to do. Every day I got up, I made three budgets: high, medium, and low. If I got a job that paid $19 an hour, this is what I could afford. If I got one that paid $25 an hour, this is what I could afford. And if I got one that was like, shoot the moon, here's what I could afford.

I had an idea of how much I had to get paid just to live. Three scenarios of how it could play out. So now I know what kind of job I have to look for today. And I know what I'm looking for because then I had to go network. I had to build a community in a place where there had previously not been one. The thing about the military is that it's an instant community. You all have this shared experience of moving around the world, and you have a limited amount of time in that place before you get to move to the next place. So, you make friends fast, love them hard, have all the fun, and then carry them with you to the next place. But here I was in this new place, and no one had that same experience. They were not interested in adding new friends to their friend cards. Their friend card was full. So, I had to figure that out myself. I set metrics for myself every day. We need food, shelter, and transportation, and I've got to make money.

Q: You've got to make money. That's right.
DK: So that was my focus. And from there, I set metrics. I'm going to apply for 50 jobs every day. I'm going to talk to three new strangers every day. I am going to remember the names of the strangers that I talk to, and I'm going to make sure that when I leave that person and someone walks up to them and says, "hey, who were you just talking to?" That was Dele Downs Kooley, and she just moved here from Germany with her family. She's looking for a house, and a job, and she is looking for other opportunities to connect with people. Those were the three data points that I wanted people to remember about me. So that's what I made sure I highlighted in my conversations with them. I had lots of fun getting to know them because I'm all about connections. My superpower is connecting people to create magic.

To do that, I need to understand what you need. So, it wasn't all about me. I needed a house, a job, a car, and a network, but I was all about, tell me about yourself, what's happening in your life, what's important to you. It was about being able to create value, because as you're getting to know and create a network, now you're meeting other people and maybe someone you met knows someone else, and now you can connect them, and you've created value.

Q: Right. What would you tell a woman who is trying to start all over again or really trying to create magic for herself? What should she do first?
DK: The first thing I would say is that you have everything that you need within you to make magic. You have to believe that first. You have everything within you to make whatever dream it is that you have a reality. You have to know and own that.

And you have to get really clear on your why, because that is what will carry you through. If you don't know why you're doing this, if you don't believe that you can do this, you will fail before you even get started, because that's the way that the human mind works. We create one of three results. We either mirror it, we seek evidence, or we actually just prove it right. To understand why you are doing this, why you want this. Your why won't be my why. You have to physically feel it in your body. It may take time for you to generate that but getting clarity on your why and having clarity on the fact that you do have everything within you, is the first thing.

Q: I know a lot of people are going to be listening to this conversation thinking about their lifestyle, thinking about what they're doing now, and whether it's really what they want. Maybe they have other options. So how can people find you and your coaching services?
DK: Yes! They can find me at delekooleycoaching.com or email dele@delekooleycoaching.com. I'm also on Instagram @delekooleycoaching.

Q: I love it. Dele, this has been amazing. I'm excited to have you as a part of the Women Who Boss Up project and to get to know you more. Thank you so much for being here.
DK: Thank you. I am so excited because what I really want to do is help other people create pivots in their life so that they can create more joy, more abundance, and more of all the things that are important to them. Thank you so much for having me here so that I can reach more people to create more magic!

DELE KOOLEY

www.delekooleycoaching.com

Dele Downs Kooley (sounds like Deli) is the master of the pivot! She has a diverse background that includes 20 years as an Air Force family member and Department of Defense civilian, working at three law enforcement agencies, and navigating corporate America at some of the largest names in the business. Her career roles centered on communications, training, finance, program management, and leadership & development.

As a certified career + life coach, she uses the lessons she learned along the way to help her clients find clarity on the life they want to live, create intentional pivots, and how to achieve their goals as quickly as possible. She speaks often on the topics of personal development, career transitions, mentoring, resilience, Diversity & Inclusion, and inclusive hiring at companies such as Amazon, Expedia Group, Microsoft, the Women in Tech Regatta, and The Bicycle Leadership Conference.

Dele's superpower is networking and connecting people to create magic! When not working or coaching her clients to create the life of their dreams this busy mother of five can be found outside enjoying the Pacific Northwest or at a live sporting event with her family.

> Had I not been open to thinking about my life differently, I never would've had the courage to do it. Mindset is everything. The thoughts that you have will create your results.
>
> —*Dele Kooley*

It's your choice to live a good story. It's your choice if you want to live out loud.

—Christine Santori

CHRISTINE SANTORI
*LimeLife by Alcone; Personal Touch Welcome;
Town Planner Calendar - Owner, Mompreneur*

CHAPTER 5

Don't Reinvent the Wheel, Know What You Want and See How Everyone do it
with Christine Santori

HEY THERE, SUPERWOMEN. I AM SO EXCITED today to have my next guest. I met her at an event last year, and I loved her enthusiasm and sense of humor. She was so funny and fun. I knew she would be amazing as a part of this Boss Up movement. Since then, I've come to learn a little bit more about her businesses. She's a multi-talented entrepreneur from Connecticut who has been in business for about seven years. She has a very inspiring story, which is part of the point of creating this Boss Up community. There's something for all of us to be able to do and be inspired by or supportive of as we go through our own entrepreneurial journeys.

Q: Christine Santori, how are you?
Christine Santori: I'm awesome! Thank you for that introduction. I hope I can live up to that.

Q: Yes. I know you're doing a lot of different things and you're building your businesses, like a lot of us are. Let's start off with what encouraged you to become an entrepreneur in the first place?
CS: Necessity! Not just financial necessity but my emotional well-being; my sanity. I am the mom of a child with both intellectual and physical disabilities. I think every mom loses herself in her kids to one degree or another, but if you have a special-needs child, you lose yourself exponentially. So I was definitely looking for something. I knew my alimony would not last forever, I knew I could be more than a mom and a special-needs mom. I knew immersing myself in something besides motherhood would give me a different sense of purpose and achievement, and that there were several more chapters of my story that had yet to be written and all I had to do was pick up the proverbial pen! So, like so many with the entrepreneurial spirit, I tossed my hat in the MLM ring! A typical 9-5 job would not have worked for me. So, I found something that did.

Q: I've seen you and your son on social media, and you guys are so cute. Just the way you include him in your social media posts is very inspiring. I love that you're able to find a reason to get out there and be visible, because it's inspiring to other people, to show that you can build a business, you can be a mom, you can be a special needs mom, and thrive as well. I love that. Tell me a little bit about your businesses and what you do.

CS: Seven-and-a-half years ago, I joined this fledgling beauty brand that nobody had ever heard of. It was a startup. That was my first business venture. Now it's a multi-million-dollar company called LimeLife by Alcone. It is available in nine countries and it's doing fantastic. In the beginning, when it was a startup, I was also just starting out and it was complete havoc. But we grew together over the years and I'm still here because I love the products and I love the community. So, my first foray into working was getting a hobby job, a side job, one of those direct-sales, MLM jobs that everyone shunned prior to COVID. Now, of course there is a major shift in attitude, boosted by billion dollar global retailers like L'Occitane, opening their own social retail sales channels. I guess I was ahead of the curve on that one!

But, really, I'm so glad I did this because I morphed from a social seller to an omni seller... Meaning that I am everywhere. Social selling was yesterday, now it's omni selling. I am selling through multiple channels, online, mobile app, desktop, print, and I sell in person. Everybody tried virtual because of Covid; now we're back in person, belly-to-belly, doing pop-ups, vendor events, one-on-ones, and trade shows.

I can be sitting on a plane and I'll just take out one of

my brushes or my lipstick and, boom, I'm selling. We're always selling. And it hit me that selling wasn't a bad thing! Actually, we are all selling something all the time. You go to doctors and you are selling yourself and your child to get the best care. You really are. You have to dress a certain way, speak a certain way; you have to sell yourself because if you don't you will be treated accordingly. So, really, you're selling, sharing, and marketing every day whether you realize it or not.

Q: I love it. Because you're naturally very bubbly, and so you present yourself that way. And it's probably very easy for you to sell because of your relationship-building and ability to talk to people and get them excited. So that's your first business. And by the way, I was in a network marketing business, too. Loved it. I was in it for 10 years. Most of the things I learned about modern entrepreneurship came from that experience. Personal development as well, because in that kind of business you have to really work on your mindset. So what's your second business?
CS: A couple of years after I joined LimeLife by Alcone, I met this lovely, cute little old lady who had a "greeting company" or a "welcoming business" and she was ready to retire. With a basket in hand, she would go door-to-door and visit new residents that moved into the area. In her basket of goodies she would give residents, for example, a pen from ACE and let them know that is a great place to go and get your oil changed. She gave new movers coupons, brochures and promotional products from local businesses and gave them a face-to-face welcome to the area. It was a wonderful tradition that she started in our town.

But she was almost 80 and ready to retire and she wanted

to sell the business. And I saw an opportunity! It was such a great fit because of my fiancé, David's advertising & SWAG business, Design|Brand|Promote, and this could also act as a funnel for my LimeLife sales. It's also something that I wanted to do because she worked the business with her husband. And I wanted to do something with David. He said to me, "Definitely do it; it makes sense. You're the face of the business. You're the social one. You go out and talk to people, and I will be in the back office, designing, invoicing and we will do this together." And I said, "Great. Let's do it." And we did, and then four months later, Covid hit.

Q: Oh, wow. But you know what? I love that idea because there are so many ways you can reach out to people, get connected to people, and help them when they first move into a city. I can attest to this, because I just moved. You don't know anything! So this is a really good way for the businesses in your town to get connected to the new people and the new people to get connected to the businesses. Such a great idea.

CS: Yes! When people ask what I do I say I'm a connector. I say that I make connections. I could be connecting over lipstick or I could be connecting about, "Oh, your oil heater is broken? I know who you should talk to." So that's how it started. But then with Covid—I had rubber gloves on, I had a mask on, we would leave packages on the porch and have residents leave it outside for 48 hours, like people were doing with groceries. Anything to avoid getting sick.

But necessity is the mother of invention, right? We were not going to let Covid slow us down. We just bought Personal Touch Welcome, a business based on face-to-face interaction and Covid had made that almost impossible.

What can we do to remedy that? David said, I'm going to create an app for this business. We're going to be like Groupon (without the fees to the businesses), we're going to be touchless, because right now we can't personally touch anything. It was brilliant!

So now we have everything on an app, and all those businesses that came to me and said "Introduce me to the new people" are now on the app, along with valued community information. People can just download it, they can show the digital coupons once they are at the shops, and they don't have to touch anything. It has worked out beautifully. So although we lost people during Covid and it was a horrible dark time for our business, it forced us to get right where we wanted to be, just way sooner than we expected to be there.

Q: I love that story. Tell me about some of the difficulties you've had to navigate, whether it's in your life or your business. What are some experiences you've gone through and what have you learned from them?
CS: Those are really big questions. I want to roll you back one second, because after I bought that business and it worked out really well, I did buy another business. I bought a franchise after that.

Q: You did? I didn't know that.
CS: I bought a franchise called the Town Planner Calendar. Now I reach 41,000 homes in the Ridgefield, Danbury, Bethel, Newtown, Sandy Hook, and Redding area by mailing this beautiful calendar to 41,000 homes. Again, connecting. The calendar goes to all my residents, and inside the calendar are the businesses who want to use a paper coupon or who want a presence every month to get their

brand recognition out there. It could be a funeral home, a real estate office, a medical practice that just wants their brand to grow or a retail store that wants to offer coupons to drive traffic to their business.

It's a resource that people get every single year, which in itself leads to challenges. Because now, imagine you're a special needs mom, that's your full-time job, your first job. Now you're doing your beauty business then you're doing this welcome service, and now you just bought a franchise and you have a deadline, a drop-dead deadline in November. It has to be done! As we say, the calendar's got to be put to bed and it's got to go to print.

That brings up a lot of challenges. And one of them is how do you scale your business? That's something that I can definitely learn from you. It's like, we're still the same two people. And now we took on all this stuff that seemed like a good idea, the businesses are all inter-connected in some way, they're all about networking and connecting business to customers, it all makes sense. But how many hours are in a day?

Q: That is always the question.
CS: Right. Time management is definitely something that challenges us. And I think it's very common because of something Mary Dougherty said to me when she approached me to lead the women's empowerment group B.I.G. (Believe Inspire Grow). I said to Mary, "Oh, gosh, why are you asking me to lead this pod?" And she said, "Well, I find the busiest people. If you want to get something done, ask them to do it!"

Q: Very, very true!

CS: So getting back to your previous question, the biggest difficulty I've had to face in my life and in my business, is being the primary caregiver for a child with special needs. I do have to work on time management, and scaling the businesses, but the real hurdle is FEAR. Always having this impending worry and gloom on my shoulders, wondering "Is everything going to be OK?" It has to do with health (his and mine) and financial security. Is everything going to be okay with my son now, and what about in the future when I'm not here?

Honestly, you talked about personal development with a direct marketing company. It's like personal development with a paycheck, as they say. I feel like the mindset, the work that I have to do to choose to get up every day, to be happy and peppy every day—it's my choice. I want to live out loud, I want to live a good story, I have all these aspirations. I must choose not to let myself get curled up in the blankets and just be boohoo, boohoo. Why him? Why me? Why now? It's never going to work out. What am I going to do for the future? I'm so worried. How am I going to work when I'm taking care of him 24/7?

That's why he's in all my videos. That's why he comes to work with me. It's really a necessity. I had to build my life around him and his needs. I want other moms to know they can choose their mindset, and they can have support too. You did ask me what I learned and I might be jumping the gun a little bit, but while I'm thinking about it: I learned that asking for help is not a bad thing. It's not selfish, it's not weakness.

I learned this over the years, I'm 56 now, my son is 24, so it's taken me a long time to get to this point on this road.

But if I could help anybody skip all the BS and get here, I would tell them to ask for help. Because you're actually giving the person you are asking a gift. You're giving them the opportunity to give, to help, to support. Maybe that person had no confidence before and by helping you they become empowered. Maybe that person didn't have many friends before and now you are bonded for life. You don't know everyone's story. So you can ask for help and by doing so, you are enriching their lives and your life.

Q: So good. From my experience of working with women, being a woman, there's something about asking for help. Of course, when you get older, you finally come to this place that you're talking about, Christine. But for many women, asking for help makes us feel like we're admitting to being weak or incapable. It's interesting.
CS: I think it's the same reason why people don't go to therapy when they should, to take care of their mental health. I think the stigma "you're weak" if you seek help is a terrible thing for women and men. It's a cultural problem and I don't think we are out of the woods with it.

Q: That's so true. What is inspiring or motivating you right now? You're a busy woman! You're doing a lot. It's one thing to have a big job as a special needs mom, but then have three companies on top of it.
It did help to have a little nest egg, too. So all those alimony payments you are getting, make sure you're putting some in the savings so when a good opportunity presents itself you can take advantage of that. That's a little tip from me. Some people get lifetime alimony. In my case, we agreed on 10 years. We have a very good divorce, because we are

united as parents to our older daughter, who is typical, and then to my son who has DOCC, a Disorder of the Corpus Callosum. We literally talk, text, email or call, almost every day, because we are a unified parental unit to get this young man to actualize, to have his best life.

The fact is that if my son has a bad day, I have a bad day. If he is having surgery, it's like I'm having surgery. I'm going through that with him. He's had 16 surgeries in the last 24 years. So what keeps me going, what keeps me motivated, I guess, is the hope and the promise of the future. I don't want to sound too hokey, but I think love keeps me really motivated. David and I first met in ninth grade in Brooklyn NY in 1981. I moved away, he moved away, never saw him again. Then Facebook was born and the old neighborhood started having reunions and 30 years later we are in each other's lives again.

So, if I may be so bold as to paraphrase The Queen, however long or short my life may be, I want it to be with David. I want to spend it in this type of relationship, living our best life, living out loud, trying to live a great story. I have him by my side every day, and work with him every day.

I know through Covid some couples were getting divorced. The lack of space and separation was their doom and they couldn't persevere. But that was not a change at all for us. But that's our Superpower! We were already working together from home and we got to continue to do that. And I just have a vision of very simple things, like sunshine and the beach and warm weather and being able to travel. It doesn't have to be an extravagant trip. Literally we drove in our car from Florida to Connecticut and we stopped at five beachy towns, and we just had a great time. So it doesn't have to be flashy or expensive. It's just time together and enjoying what's around. That's what really motivates me every single day. That's why I have trouble with the winter. Connecticut winters are horrible! That's why part of my plan or my dream, is to snowbird because I can do a lot of my work from wherever I am. So why not have a couple months in the winter in Florida and visit our parents and friends? Life is short and it's beautiful. And so you have to just grab it every single day.

Q: What advice would you give to another woman who really wants to be successful, who wants to get going with something entrepreneurial, maybe she has an idea or she's inspired? What's her first step?
CS: Oh, gosh. I don't want to sound like I'm plugging B.I.G (Believe, Inspire, Grow), but find a group.

Q: I agree with you.
CS: Find a group. A women's empowerment group, or another community group. We have mom's clubs in Ridgefield, we have women's clubs, we have a voters club. There are so many networks of business clubs that are probably free, that you can join to meet other women and exchange ideas. If you don't know what you want to do, this will help you sort it out by seeing what other people are doing and how they're doing it. If you already know what you want to do, then it's a little bit easier to find those networks. I would steer everyone virtual as much as possible at the beginning, because that's where you get all of your information. But then when you want to get the client, face to face.

Q: Face to face is best.
CS: You've got to go in. Knock on the doors. When we want

to fill the calendar, we go into the business in person. When I am delivering to a newcomer I go right to their door to meet them. There used to be a process of identifying them, leaving a note, if they aren't home, going back another day, and another, and finally making an appointment to visit. Nobody has any time for that. I just go, okay, there's 10 people on this road, I'm doing that this week. And I'll just knock on doors. And if I'm lucky, they're home and if I'm not lucky, they're not home and I'll go back another day.

But I think this is like a lost art. We had a speaker come into our LimeLife national conference, and he was talking about what a unique time in history we live in now. There's at least four generations alive right now. We've got Baby Boomers, Gen X, Millennials and Gen Z. Each group of people you're talking to requires a different type of voice, a different type of marketing. The young people are not comfortable with eye contact. So when you're talking to a young person and you want to get their attention, don't be all in their face. You have to know who you're talking to. And if you hand them a tablet or you hand them something to look at, so they don't have to look at you, you're actually going to be more successful selling to them.

If you are doing this with a Baby Boomer, oh, my God, forget it. They want a big smile, eye contact, and a big handshake. They want that contact, give me a hug, you know? So I would also say, know your audience. That's a big thing.

So first, sort out what you want to do. If you know what you want to do, see how everyone else is doing it. You don't have to reinvent the wheel. See what resources are available for you. And then know your audience. You're going to have to do a little bit of research to know your audience.

However you want to do it, know who your audience is because it's not everyone. They always say, if your audience is everyone, it's no one. So know who your audience is and then figure out how you're going to market to them. Ask for help, ask for help, ask for help, and believe in yourself. Because nobody else is going to believe in you if you don't believe in yourself.

Q: That's right. Christine, this has been so fun.
CS: Thank you.

Q: How can people find out more about your businesses and connect with you?
CS: The easiest way to find me is on social media with my name, Christine Santori. I'm also on Insta under @personaltouchwelcome where I run Personal Touch Welcome and Town Planner Calendar. And @perfectleeimperfect is where I have my professional makeup and all natural skin care conversations. Today I'm brand partners with LimeLife by Alcone, MyL'Occitane, and Savvi, a newish athleisure clothing brand.

Branding and rebranding is an important thing. We've had a lot of conversations in our B.I.G. group about it, because there are so many women who are diversified now. You could be a social seller and partner with 10 different brands, like influencers and micro-influencers do, and you wonder, "How do I select a business name?" It makes the most sense to just use your own name if possible.

Q: Use your own name, yes.
CS: Yes, I would put everything under one umbrella, in your own name from the beginning.

Q: Christine, thank you. I look forward to all the stuff that we're going to be doing together.

CS: Thank you Tam! The future is going to be so exciting.

CHRISTINE SANTORI

"I am a Special Needs MOM, full time primary caregiver to 24 year old son with physical and intellectual disabilities.

I am an Entrepreneur w LimeLife 8 years - direct selling/social selling/ OMNI SELLING. Purchased our first company at age 53 PTW, and our second company at age 55 TP.

I am a CONNECTOR, micro influencer...

BIG, Chamber, Commission for Accessibility, Gala Committees for KIC, SPHERE, Ridgefield Playhouse. Donate to NODCC for Sean and families like ours."

At the end of the day, I believe in the sheer power of believing in yourself. Don't let yourself be your own worst enemy.

—Joanne Whitlock

JOANNE WHITLOCK
United States Air Force
U.S. Air Force Officer & DEI Advocate

CHAPTER 6

Don't Let Yourself be your Own Hindrance to your Progress and Success
with Joanne Whitlock

HEY THERE, SUPERWOMEN. I AM SO EXCITED today to have my next guest. I don't know if I say this very often, but I was in the military, in the Reserves. It's been a long time now, I was in the Army. And it's such a different world for me, such a different time in my life. But I went into the military right after high school, and it just kind of changed my life. I think it did affect the way I do things and my ability to now focus on my life. I definitely picked up a lot of great traits by going through basic training and all this. I'm excited to have my next guest because she is a Captain in the United States Air Force. An amazing, decorated Captain who worked in forensics before she went into the military. I love to meet a woman who is succeeding in what you might think of as a male-dominated career. And so this is going to be a really fun conversation because tomorrow she's moving into a whole other job. So let's get into it.

Q: Ms.—or I should say Captain—Joanne Whitlock, how are you?
Joanne Whitlock: Hey, Tam, I'm good. Thank you so much for having me. I'm so honored to be part of your movement, I'm honored to be part of your program, and very happy to be here. So thank you.

Q: I really am excited about this. Tell me a little about your background. I know that you were born and raised in Manila, in the Philippines, and you went through Air Force Officer Training School in 2013. What made you go into the military in the first place? You had been a forensics investigator in the civilian sector.
JW: I was born and spent my early childhood in the Philippines with my family, and then my later childhood and early adulthood in Florida. My dad—my stepdad, but he's my dad—he's from Texas, adopted me, my brother, and my sister. He is a Vietnam War veteran. He flew C-130s, so that was a big influence there. But he's the reason I'm in the United States to begin with, you know, he moved us here and gave me a better life.

Growing up in the Asian culture, especially in Filipino culture, it's ingrained in you that you're going to be a nurse, you're going to be a doctor, you're going to be a lawyer. There are just those stereotypes that are very prevalent in our culture. And I kind of went along with it until I got into high school. Then I realized that was not really what I wanted to do.

I got my Bachelor's Degree in Biological Anthropology and my Master's in Forensic Science. And actually I did that for a few years in the Washington, D.C., area. I was a Forensic Investigator. But the huge military pull from my family was still very much there. My brother and sister joined the Air Force and followed in my dad's footsteps. It's definitely a long military legacy, and so eventually I decided to commission in the Air Force, initially wanting to do something similar, but I ended up in a completely different field. Now I'm a Logistics Readiness Officer by trade. That is my career field in the military.

I've been in the Air Force for about 10 years now. I've been deployed to Africa, the Middle East, and been stationed at various locations across the U.S. and overseas. It's been a fun ride. So there was a lot of family influence along with really wanting to give back to a country that's done so much for me and my family, especially from our very, very humble beginnings in the Philippines.

Q: Very cool. A lot of people do follow their parents into the military. My dad was in the military. I wasn't raised by my dad, but he was in the military and I have plenty of uncles that served. My brother went in as well. It wasn't like there was pressure on me at all, but it certainly wasn't a foreign idea. What would you say are the best things that you learned? I alluded to how much I personally learned as a human being by going into the military. What are some highlights of your experience?

JW: The military has given me great opportunities to travel, and that is a big part of me. I love traveling and learning more about other cultures. I've been all over the world, all over the country. So experiencing that and just opening up my eyes to different cultures, different perspectives, and different walks of life, were highlights.

And what's so great about the military is you come together with people from all walks of life and people that you go to training with become lifelong friends, even though they may have nothing in common with you. The biggest thing that I've enjoyed about the military is learning about where everybody has come from and what brought them to the military, kind of like what you're asking me now. Everybody has such a different origin story of how they got to where they are. And it's incredible.

And then most of what I've learned about leadership and being a supervisor is from the military. Those were my formative career years, in the military. So I learned the dos and don'ts of being a leader. I have definitely experienced leaders whose footsteps I would never follow. And I have also experienced leaders that I aim to emulate. So the military helped my ability to formulate my own style of leadership through all that experience.

Q: That's incredible. What challenges have you experienced in your life or in your career? We all go through ups and downs. What are some of the things you've had to persevere through?

JW: The hardest thing that I've experienced in my personal life is that my mother passed away when I was 15. That was definitely a life-changing event for me. Those are formative years, when you would want to have your mother there. So that has influenced a lot of things about me and about how I grew up. Also, as I mentioned, my brother and sister were also in the military, so we were spread around the globe quite a bit, even though we are extremely, extremely close. So we don't get to see each other every holiday. We don't get to have those reunions all the time. That's also a challenge in my personal life.

Career-wise, if you really want to get into it, when I was a Forensic Investigator, I worked with detectives often. So that was a very male-dominated environment.

Q: Oh, yeah.

JW: And then I transitioned to the military, an even more male-dominated career. So, yeah, being exposed to that and the accumulation of all the various experiences of being dismissed as a female, as a minority. I'm 5'2", I'm an Asian female. I'm not physically imposing, my voice is not loud, so it's easy for me to be overlooked or disregarded. When I was in a room, I'd look around and, you know, one of these things is not like the other. I'm usually the only one that looks like me. In the beginning, I used to just allow myself to blend in. Looking back, I think having that mindset may have caused me to experience some imposter syndrome during certain parts of my life and my career and through my successes.

And then just the feelings of being dismissed slowly creeping up along with micro-aggressions and racial jokes. I kind of went along with it because it was the easy thing to do. But I still experience that 10 years in. So yeah, it's tough sometimes.

Q: It's tough. You're a minority woman in a very male-dominated place, so you're probably dealing with things from all sides, even if you just let it roll off your back, it isn't easy. Most of my career was in a male-dominated industry as a Black female—now, I'm the opposite of you, I'm 5'11", so, you know, I can kind of look him in the face. That's a little bit easier for me.

JW: When I was in my early 20s as an Investigator, I had male detectives say, "You're too pretty for this line of work." That's how I started off. And then, like I said, when I went to the military, I was extremely male-dominated. I had lunch with a coworker one time, we're both in our military uniforms. Somebody comes up to our table and thanks my coworker for his service, does not even acknowledge me at all. We are sitting right there together, we are sitting in uniform together. Or I go to the DMV or another agency where I need to either apply for military status or veteran status and I have been told several times, "Oh, sorry, ma'am, the military member is the one that needs to be present to get this benefit" or something like that. Or I'm moving for a military assignment, so I have the moving company at my house, packing up my belongings, and they ask me, "So how long has your husband been in the military? Where is he getting stationed to know that you guys are moving?" And I'm like, "It's me. I'm a military member."

Q: Wow.
JW: The constant exposure to those preconceptions and being disregarded just eventually wears you down.

Q: It does. What is the new assignment? What are you going to be doing now?
JW: I'm relocating to Southern California. I'm going to be an Assistant Professor of Aerospace Studies and Operations Officer for Cal State University in San Bernardino for the Air Force ROTC program there.

Q: That is so cool.
JW: I am very stoked. I will be directly influencing and developing the next generation of officers that are coming after me. It's all the college students who are enrolled in Air Force ROTC, I'll be leading and guiding them into their commissioning into the military.

Q: How long is that assignment?
JW: At least two years, potentially three.

Q: That has to be exciting.
JW: I am very excited about it. Especially being out west, that's really where I feel more at home. Most of my family live in Las Vegas. There's also quite a bit more diversity than where I currently am, in Charleston, South Carolina. It is night and day. So, yes, I'm very excited. And just having that direct hand in developing tomorrow's Air Force leaders is very, very exciting for me.

Q: What motivates you, or what is inspiring you right now?
JW: I get motivated when I see statistics and data that show how Asian females, females, minorities, are not widely represented in the military. So as of last year, September 2021, the active duty Air Force only comprised about 5 percent Asian Americans, Native Hawaiians and Pacific Islanders. And then obviously significantly less so for Asian females. So wanting to see that representation and wanting to see more of us in senior, higher-ranking positions is really what motivates me.

I'm actually part of this Barrier Analysis Working Group within the Air Force that's focused on analyzing the barriers to promotion and recruitment of Asian Americans in the military. What is hindering that? And I get motivated by those pioneers in the Asian American Pacific Islander and Native Hawaiian communities who came before me and those who are going to come after me. I know I follow in the footsteps of those pioneers, and I know that things I do right now are going to influence those that are going to come after me. So that influence definitely motivates me, and I stand on the shoulders of those before me.

Knowing that I can pave the path for those who are coming after me, that's a huge motivation. And I refuse to let that next generation down, which is why I'm super excited about this assignment. I stay motivated by talking to peers, mentors, and loved ones and seeing the slow change—I say slow because it is a very slow change—seeing that there is impact, there is effect. That's what motivates me the most.

Q: That's awesome. What would you say to another female, minority female, Asian female, to help her be successful in any endeavor? What is the main thing, do you think?

JW: This is funny because I actually just said this to somebody. I'm a mentor with Big Brother, Big Sister for teenage youth, for minority females. And I was just having dinner with one of my mentees yesterday and I told her, because she's going through high school right now, I told her, "Force the world to tell you no, and then keep going anyway."

Admittedly, I still do battle with that sometimes. I still get into my own head and sometimes want to give up or think that I don't have what it takes when certain opportunities arise or I don't have the skill set. But at the end of the day I believe in the sheer power of believing in yourself.

So I told her, "Don't let yourself be your own worst enemy or be the hindrance to your own progress and success." I think people fall into that trap quite a bit. We get into our own heads and then we are the ones that end up being our own barrier towards advancement. So boldly take on the world, force them to tell you no, and then make it your goal to prove them wrong.

Q: I love that.

JW: I truly, truly believe that we have everything in ourselves. We already have, within ourselves, everything we need to be successful, to be exactly what we need. It's just a matter of getting that out there. One of my favorite quotes from Maya Angelou says, "You alone are enough." You have nothing to prove to anybody. And I do believe that.

Q: I do too. I really do. Oh, my goodness, Joanne, I am so excited to have you as part of this project. Is there anything else that you would like to share with my audience?
JW: Right now I am super excited to be part of this project, because, again, I am trying to advance my efforts in DEI. I am very passionate after the experiences that I just explained to you, over 10 years accumulating that feeling. I've seen in myself the internal evolution of my voice, wanting my voice heard. I no longer doubt whether I belong or whether my skills are enough. I used to shy away from speaking up and all that. Now, when I stick out in the room, rather than trying to blend in I view the fact that I stick out as a positive thing.

I eagerly provide my insight and different perspectives. I consider myself a strong advocate for DEI, empowering minorities and women within the military and outside. This past May, I led Asian American Pacific Islander Heritage Month for the entire Air Force. We did a lot of great interviews and efforts with that. It was a fantastic month.

And the passion for that is also why I'm a mentor for Big Brother, Big Sister. I sit on the Executive Board for a nonprofit organization that's based out of San Diego, the Asian Culture and Media Alliance. They're focused on supporting and empowering the AANHPI community through media arts and entertainment. So there are lots of efforts that I'm getting involved in and that I'm part of. And now your project! I'm stoked, stoked, stoked to meet and network with so many incredible women, to learn from them and to network.

Q: I love it. I love all the stuff that you're doing. You got more involved in DEI and it led to the next thing and the next thing. As you open up and share your voice, you empower other women to share their voices. You give them permission to share. And I just love what you're creating. How can people connect with you?

JW: I am very active on LinkedIn, Joanne-Whitlock. I'm a big networker there, so I reach out to folks there all the time and vice versa. My email is jmwhitlock11@gmail.com and I'm very happy to connect, network, and discuss future efforts and events with people.

Q: Thank you, Captain Whitlock, for being here. I look forward to talking to you again and all the stuff we're going to be doing this year.

JW: Yes. Thank you, Tam.

JOANNE WHITLOCK

Born and raised in Manila, Philippines before relocating to Florida, Joanne is now an active duty Logistics Readiness Officer in the United State Air Force. She is a staunch advocate for diversity and inclusion and promoting Asian American, Native Hawaiian and Pacific Islander (AANHPI) heritage across various platforms. She recently led the Department of the Air Force's efforts for AAPI Heritage Month and serves as a member of their Barrier Analysis Working Group where she is involved in analyzing data, trends and barriers to identify and address issues impacting AANHPI personnel in the Air Force.

Joanne is committed to supporting and empowering underrepresented communities. She serves on the Executive Board for Asian Culture and Media Alliance and is a longstanding mentor for Big Brother Big Sister. She holds a Bachelor's Degree in Biological Anthropology and a Masters Degree in Forensic

Science and was a Medicolegal Death Investigator in the Washington, DC area (Northern Virginia) prior to commissioning in the Air Force. As of September 2022, she serves as an Assistant Professor of Aerospace Studies in California State University – San Bernardino.

When we are present with our definition of success, we can enjoy the journey with ease and flow.

—Wen Hsu

WEN HSU
Wen Coaching
Founder, Chief Transformation Officer

CHAPTER 7

Knowing your Own Definition of Success
with Wen Hsu

HEY THERE, SUPERWOMEN. I AM SO EXCITED TO have my next guest. She is a certified coach. She has 15 years of experience in the tech industry. She is now really focusing on coaching and helping other first- and second-generation immigrant women to find fulfillment in their lives and in their businesses. She struggled for many years with authenticity and happiness and career growth, and a lot of it had to do with cultural differences she had to navigate through. I love this conversation because a lot of us out here can relate. You may not have dealt with the exact same situations that she has, but we all, as women especially, can relate to the struggle. The struggle of not being taken seriously and being underestimated. So let's get into this conversation.

Q: Wen Hsu, how are you?
Wen Hsu: I'm good. Thank you, Tam, for the awesome introduction.

Q: I've been talking more and more lately about DEI and about inclusion in many different contexts. I love the angle that you bring to that conversation. But let's start with how you came to coaching after a long career in the tech industry.
WH: I would say I am an accidental entrepreneur.

Q: A lot of us are!
WH: Yes. Coming from my Taiwanese roots, having a stable and nice-paying job is the default. It's so important. That's why I followed that path and stayed in tech for 15+ years. Being an enduring leader with a great reputation, I loved leading teams and building products in the tech industry. But in the process of climbing that career ladder, I learned to be like a typical leader: assertive, extroverted, and aggressive. As I continued to progress, I felt like I left part of myself feeling rejected in the process. Being in the leadership role also taught me how much politics and ego really can change a company, how they can turn something from really great to bad.

So I wasn't really fulfilled at the time. I wanted to be authentic and bring a massive impact, but I didn't know how. To help, I hired a coach. Ever since then, my life has changed completely—my work life, personal life, and, most important, my relationship with myself. My first inquiry was really to get to know myself deeply. It also was the first time that I was able to say yes to myself, by taking a year-long sabbatical to really explore who I am, what I want, etc. Given my own experience being coached, I knew quickly that was the kind of impact I desired to bring to others.

So I went through a fairly robust coaching program to get certified, and started to coach on top of a full-time tech job at a startup. Since working in tech is so lucrative, many people have the thought that they want to get financial freedom so they don't have to work for money. My original plan was to stay in tech and get to financial freedom maybe in five to eight years such that I wouldn't have the pressure of coaching being my main source of income. Of course, we all know things in life don't always work out as planned.

Q: That's right.
WH: I actually got laid off in 2021 after a senior leader was brought into the company. The company was at its peak, its highest valuation, everything looked great, so I was really shocked that it happened. Also, considering my roots, I think external validation had been quite important to me, so the experience was like a slap in the face. Like I was not good enough for someone even though he doesn't even know me.

So I took three months off and in the end kind of realized it's not really about me. I pretty much just witnessed politics again at work. So I had choices. I could go back to tech fairly easily given my reputation and connections, but in my heart, I just didn't feel like it. I didn't have that motivation to work for someone else, ask for permission, or follow other people's rules anymore. I already had paying clients at the time, so I knew people were willing to pay for my service. But when I thought, "OK, let me do coaching full time," the thought itself actually terrified me.

Q: Right.

WH: Because in the past few years I've become a pretty good coach, but I didn't focus on the business side of coaching. I knew nothing about growing a business, so it is a very unconventional path for me. However, I had gained the clarity of what I really wanted once I reached financial freedom, and that is to coach more and to be with my family more. My entire family is still in Taiwan and I want to travel more.

With that realization, it dawned on me: "If I go full-time coaching now, does that mean that I can have that life right now instead of waiting for five to eight years?" So with that thought, I was like, yes, I can have it now. I was so excited. So that pushed me over my own fears and the best thing is I started to see the layoff as a gift. It was a not-so-gentle nudge from the universe telling me, "Hey, Wen, you're ready, go take that next step." So I did and that's how I became an entrepreneur, having my own coaching business.

Q: I'm so glad you did. Now here I have to ask this question: You are an Asian-American woman and your parents probably were so proud that you had a really great job in tech. Then all of a sudden you decided to take the very unconventional path of coaching. What was that like?

WH: Oh, such a great question. The first thing was to convince myself, especially because of the uncertainty, the unknown. I learned to challenge what I believe in, because before, from my parents, from my social environment, we always felt that having a stable job and being in a company was the goal. Work hard, keep your head down. That's the cultural playbook that I received. I still remember when I switched jobs the first time, my dad said, "Are you sure?" So we are already in a different world where we need to constantly learn new things so we don't become stale. Even the thought that being with a company is more stable, it's just not true.

Q: It's not.
WH: So many people are let go here and there given the economy's ups and down or for no reason at all or for political reasons. It is not safe unless we truly own our own knowledge, our own wisdom, knowing what we want and going after what we want. So with that understanding, I wanted to create that reality for myself instead of relying on my environment to have it for me. That to me was the biggest mindset shift for me to really go for it wholeheartedly.

Q: Amazing. Because it's scary and I'm sure your parents were probably nervous as heck. They know what a doctor is. They know what a lawyer is. They know what computer science is, but they don't know what coaching is.
Yeah. I still have problems explaining to them. But they're happy for me.

Q: Yes, you're doing great. What are the biggest hurdles you have had to overcome, whether in your business life or your personal life?
WH: To me the most important thing is to really know who I am and to show up 100 percent. Especially being a first-time "solopreneur," there is the need for me to create clients. I've gone on many tangents with marketing experts and I've tried to learn from others, but I found out there are so many "shoulds" in those programs that are not really for me. It's similar to how I got lost in the corporate world trying to mimic what worked for others. I tried to follow all those

"shoulds"—how I should present myself, how I should craft my image. It just didn't work for me. So for a few months I wasn't actually making any money, and of course I got more stressed. So I learned the hard way that to grow my business, there is no sure path and I really need to know who I am and how I want to truly show up in the world.

Q: That's right. So good.
WH: It's a process of really discovering and doing deep work. So I now take the time to create values for others before they even become my clients. I learned to grow my coaching business one deep conversation at a time. Not to get clients, but to make a difference. That can really change how I approach people. Especially now, in a world where people have short attention spans and everything everywhere is trying to get your attention. But a lot of that is at the surface level, and I realized people crave that deep connection with people who truly are interested in them, can see them, and care about them, and that's where I come in. I'm really out for build that long-term relationship.

All my clients now are coming by direct invitation or referral only because I let that coaching experience with me actually do the selling for me. I want that experience to be so good they never forget it. I want to stay in my zone of genius, not do marketing. I want to hire other people to do that in their own zone of genius. I want to stay seeing the sparks in my clients and help them get to places that they don't even know possible. So I actually have many people come back to me months or a year after our first conversation when they're really ready to work with me. Growing my business this way has been so much more fun and I feel much more at ease and in flow. Every day I just think about what differences I like to make.

Q: I love that philosophy of coaching.
WH: It's just a natural way to view my coaching business.

Q: It's a very good way because it also keeps you authentic, focused on what you're doing, focused on the person, and not focus on the money. The money is important, of course, but you have to start with being connected to what the client really needs and wants. What advice would you give to an entrepreneur who wants more success? What would you tell them to think about first?
WH: I've thought about this a lot because most people come to me, and success is what they want. People come to me with all different ideas of success. The first advice I will give is to define what being successful looks like to you. Because many of us form our ideas of success based on how success is defined by society, our boss, our friends, or our parents. But what is your own definition of success?

Also, I would add the word "being": What does *being successful* look like to you? It is important because oftentimes when we think about success, we think it's out there in the distance. We don't get to "success" unless we put in ten years of effort. It's something that you need to grind now to get later. So we don't live in the now and we miss the present moment.

But when we are present to our own definition of being successful, then we can enjoy the journey with ease and flow. Let me give you a few of my own definitions. I know I'm successful when I can wake up every day and ask, "What difference would I like to make today?" I know I'm successful when I can be with my family for a month every year. I know I'm being successful when my revenue exceeds my lifestyle needs. The list goes on, but just knowing my own definitions of a successful life really helped me. I took a month off this summer to be with my family for my younger sister's wedding. Instead of feeling anxious about not working, not having that income, I'm like, "Oh, my God, I actually achieved my own definition of success." That made me so happy.

Q: There's something you wrote, and I want to repeat it here because it's so good. You wrote, "You don't need confidence. What you need is courage to take tiny actions." I thought, yes, I'm going to use that for the rest of my life.
WH: Thank you for bringing that up. After I wrote that, my second thought was, but we need to know where we want to get to first, right?

Q: That's true.
WH: The first thing is to know where we want to go, and the second is taking the steps to get there. I really feel this one. We don't need confidence. What we need is the courage to take tiny steps. I don't know if you remember, Tam, when we were young girls, we were fearless. We danced like nobody was watching and we fell, we giggled, we stood up, and then we tried again. Everything was so fun. Somehow in the way of becoming adults, we lost that. The fear of failure and rejection really prevented us from showing up.

Sometimes we don't even try so we actually fail ahead of time. This is what I learned throughout this business journey. So many things I do right now are new to me, and I don't really need to know how to do them because I know as long as I take that step, then I will eventually get to where I want to go, and I will receive the confidence. That's the process of doing it. So confidence is actually the result. Those outcomes of taking tiny steps, they are all information to help us make the best decision about what's next. Take those tiny steps, test, learn, adjust, and test again. Also, most important, have tons of fun in the process.

Q: How do you stay motivated? I'm sure it's difficult when you're a coach. For me, I'm often taking on the energy of the people that I'm talking to while I'm going through my own ups and downs. Entrepreneurship can have high highs and low lows. It's a very interesting journey. So how do you stay motivated?
WH: The first mindset shift for me as a coach was to realize that no one needs to be saved.

Q: So good.
WH: That takes the pressure off me, because I'm not here to save anybody. I'm here to help you create the life that you want. So I'm motivated whenever I'm in touch with my purpose. For right now that purpose is to help first- and second-generation immigrant women leaders to design and reach career and life success as they define it for themselves. Given my own experience and the cultural playbook that we talked about, it's very easy for us to be small, waiting to be seen and working super hard. I experienced myself and heard from so many other immigrant women leaders about stereotyping, sexism, and ageism that come into play in society and in corporate especially against women of color. And then on top of it we can be our own worst enemy, the worst inner critic to ourselves such that we enforce super high standards on ourselves. The common thing I see in people is that we need to be perfect even when we do things for the first time. We always feel the need to know the answer and give that answer with a smile.

Q: That's so true.
WH: Yes, it brings some success, but I know so many people in very high positions feeling lost, being unhappy and unfulfilled. We don't really have to operate this way. Like I say, I'm here to help people create—create that possibility, create that freedom that they have in their life already but that currently might be covered up by all the "shoulds" and other constraints. I imagine a world where we all get to write our own playbook, our own rules, so we create and reach our success.

I also believe that when we have more diverse and successful women at the top, the corporate culture is going to change. The egos don't always win, and the world can really be changed for the better. Whenever I think about that, I just feel pushed to do so many things to be seen, to be known, so that I can help all those women be part of the mission to make this world better.

Q: Wen, I love this conversation. I love your mission and where you're going. What is the easiest way for people to connect with you or to find out more about your coaching?
WH: My website is wencoaching.com and I am Wen Coaching on LinkedIn as well.

Q: Thank you. This has been so fun and I look forward to all the stuff we're going to be doing in the next year.
WH: Thank you, Tam. This has been so much fun for me also.

WEN HSU

Wen Hsu is 1st generation Taiwanese American, founder and Chief Transformation Officer at Wen Coaching.

After working 15 years as an engineering leader in the tech industry, Wen became known for her strategic thinking, building self-sustainable teams, and creating empathetic leaders. Yet, she experienced the constraints and hurdles immigrant female leaders face first hand. She lost herself in the process of climbing corporate America and was exhausted from working hard to prove herself again and again.

Thankfully, through deep inner work, courage, and coaching, she found her way back to herself. She learns to have courage to take tiny actions to reach her impossible goals. She realizes that worthiness is a birthright without having to hustle for it. She consciously challenges the *"cultural playbook"* she received and creates her own rules in life.

Now, her passion is to help immigrants, aspiring female leaders to dream, design, and reach their own definition of success in career and life. In the process of achieving their impossible goals, people will have more confidence, freedom, and fulfillment as a result.

YOU'RE ALWAYS ONE DECISION AWAY FROM A TOTALLY DIFFERENT LIFE

TIME TO BOSSUP!

SECTION 2
Health

DR. TEISHA ROBERTSON
TaylorFit For You, LLC
CEO and Owner

CHAPTER 8

Digging Deep in to Your Superficial Why's
with Dr. Teisha Robertson

HEY THERE, SUPERWOMEN. I AM SO EXCITED TO have my next guest. She is an amazing certified online health and wellness coach, Dr. Teisha Robertson. The name of her company is Taylor Fit For You. And she has created a safe and supportive space for busy, overwhelmed women to level up their health through what she calls "taylor-fit" goals. I love that because when I think about my own fitness and health journey—I was also a health coach for about 10 years—but as we get older or as we get busier, a lot of times we think about everybody else, we don't always think about ourselves. So I like the idea of a program being tailored for individuals because everybody has a different lifestyle, right? And so I'm really excited to have you here.

Q: Dr. Teisha Robertson, how are you?
Dr. Teisha Robertson: I am doing awesome. This week is just flying by you know, I looked up and it's already Wednesday. Thank you so much for having me. I really appreciate this opportunity because any way that I'm able to share on a platform about health and wellness, I am there.

Q: Health is one of the things that is a pillar for a businesswoman. There was a time that spent so much energy focusing everywhere else that it led to some health issues. So anytime I get a chance to tell people to make this a priority, I do. So I'm so glad to have you as well. Tell me a little bit about your background. How did you get into fitness?
TR: I was born and raised in Trinidad and growing up, the staple foods there that I would always eat were rice, bread, pasta, and milk. Growing up, that's what had to be on my plate. And literally everything else was second rate. When it comes to vegetables, what are vegetables? At a young age, no, I was not having it. And then in terms of proteins—of course, I didn't know that's what it was called back then—it had to be fried fish or curry chicken or types of food that were higher in fat. Growing up, I was a heavier child. At the age of 10, I developed stretch marks. And being a 10-year-old with stretch marks really turned my world upside down because, first of all, I have to walk around with this, not realizing this was something that was going to be permanent at the time.

My mom tried everything. I was taken to every single dermatologist, nothing helped. So growing up a heavier child, stretch marks and all, I got to the point where I just went to school, came home, ate, slept, and repeat. Went to school, came home, ate, and slept. That was it. I wasn't involved in any sports, any activities at a younger age. I did no form of movement, no activity, and I was still eating those types of foods. So I continued to gain weight until I got to my heaviest at over 200 pounds at the age of 14 and 15. I wanted to lose weight so I tried every single thing under the sun. You name it, if it was out there, I tried it, from pills to wearing a sauna suit to just doing juicing for a few days. Each time, the weight kept coming back and coming back. And then I eventually would just feel like giving up because nothing was working.

The real turning point was when my mom developed diabetes and high blood pressure. I had started pharmacy school and at the time I had found out that I was pre-hypertensive. And when you find this out and then your mom also develops high blood pressure and diabetes, it's like a whirlwind spins.

I wasn't the heaviest of my life when I was in pharmacy school, but I was doing things that were not healthy. I would still eat what I wanted to eat, and then I would do cardio for an hour every single day. But my cholesterol was high and my blood pressure was also high because when you fuel your body with the wrong foods and you think, "Oh, I'm working it off, I'm exercising it off," it's like being counter-productive to being healthy. I was able to lose the weight, but I wasn't doing it in a healthy way for my life, for my heart.

So this is what really got me into my mindset spiral, where I started to learn more about proper eating, what is a protein, what is fat, what is a carb, what are the macros? How do I need to eat in order to sustain my lifestyle as well as my heart health? How can I help my mom to do the same? So that is how my background led me to my life today.

Q: That is so cool. So you went to pharmacy school, so you are a pharmacist right now?
TR: I am a pharmacist, yes.

Q: And then you also have this fitness business, which is your passion or side hustle. And you are really focused on growing this brand to help more people to get serious about their health.
TR: Yes, because heart disease is the number-one killer for everyone. And of course for us, as women, we're so consumed with, as you said, that busy lifestyle, being a busy mom, a busy entrepreneur, student, business owner. The word is busy, busy. And what I find for a lot of people is that because their life is so busy, their self-care gets put on the back burner. It is not a priority.

And then many women just do not know where to start or how to start. I realized that there are just too many people getting heart disease, which is caused by obesity, high blood pressure, high cholesterol, and diabetes, and these things are controllable. We can control all four of these—unless you're a Type 1 diabetic—but otherwise, these are all disease states that we can take control of.

Q: It's about making lifestyle choices. I love this conversation. What are some obstacles that you've had to overcome in your journey of building this business? What are some of the things that you have dealt with?
TR: For me, the big obstacle was getting out of my own way. When you're trying to start a business, it can be very daunting, especially if you let others get in your ear. You have to be careful who you share your ideas with. And you also have to be careful who you let into your circle or into your space because a lot of people are not there for you,

they're there to see you fail. And because they're there to see you fail, they come in with these negative thoughts, negative voices, and that can be very discouraging.

So it took me a while. I've been a personal trainer since 2016 and I knew this is what I wanted to do, but I just didn't have the momentum. I didn't have the foresight to see that I could do it. And there were certain people who said you can't be a business owner, you don't have an entrepreneur mindset, just continue to work. Don't worry about it. Let other people handle that. Let other people do that. So the biggest obstacle for me was to just stop listening to the chitter chatter, stop listening to the talk, and know that yes, Teisha, you can do this. You just have to put your mind to it and get to it.

Q: I love that so much. Just put your mind to it and get to it. That is the most powerful thing that you could possibly say and do for yourself. How do you stay motivated? I know the first motivation was probably your own health journey. And then the second motivation was your mom's health journey. How do you continue that momentum of motivation?
TR: Motivation for me is my future, my heart health, and my kids. Wanting to be around for them is bigger than just me. Also, my motivation is how far I've come. While I still have these stretch marks, they're just a reminder of where I was and what I've accomplished. I'll be 43 this year and I am living the healthiest, happiest time of my life. And that has to do with putting myself first and my self-care first. So just seeing how my life has just come 360, now I don't listen to the negative thoughts. Now I wake up every morning speaking positivity into myself, speaking affirmations into me. Learning to put myself first has helped to get me over a lot of the obstacles, a lot of the negativity. And then that just keeps me going.

Q: I'm thinking about all of the women that really need to take time for themselves. My mom always said take time with yourself. It should not be a second thought. It is your health. Some of the statistics are daunting to think about when it comes to high blood pressure and diabetes. What advice would you give to a female entrepreneur like yourself so that she can be successful with her health or her business. What should she really do or start now?
TR: Yes! The key, as you just said, is start now. Starting now is the first step. The second step is mindset. Mindset is everything. No matter what you're doing, whether it's starting a business, whether it's starting your health journey, you have to get your mind right. Figure out your "why" in anything that you do. If you want to be an entrepreneur and you want to start a business, ask why. Why are you starting that business? If you say you want to lose weight and be a healthier version of yourself, why?

A lot of people, when they think about their "why," they come up with something that is superficial. That is not going to take you far. So dig deeper. Dig real deep and figure out what is your why. For me, my why and why I wanted to be healthy is when I looked at my mom and her developing diabetes and high blood pressure, and then me also getting that high cholesterol lab result back, that high blood pressure reading where the doctor said if you come back with high blood pressure one more time, we're putting your on medications—that is my why.

My why is deeper than I just want to look good for a wedding. Or I just want to look good for the next trip that I take. Or I just want to look good for my birthday. Because when you have those superficial whys, those days come. Your birthday comes, the wedding comes, the trip comes. And *then* what is your why? You feel like you have to start all over. So dig really deep into your why, regardless of whether it's why you're starting your business, going back to school, changing your career, what is your why? And then once you have that, that gets you to the mindset shift where you *want* to do the next steps that you have to do to get to the next level of whatever it is you are moving toward. Your health goals, your journey with entrepreneurship, going back to school, whatever. Get that why, get that mindset, and you're on your way.

Q: So good. Teisha, this has been so incredible. How can people find out more about your services? Where can they find you on social media, because I know I have listeners who are like, "Yeah, I need to talk to her."
TR: You're too kind. Thank you so much. I am very heavy on Instagram. I love to share lots of nutrition tips, workout tips that you could do in the comfort of your own home. I share workout tips you could do from bed. Yes, bed! And I love sharing alternative nutrition hacks. People say, "Oh, I love pizza." Well, guess what? There's a healthier version of pizza you can make out of chicken. So I love sharing this information with my audience on Instagram. You can connect with me @TaylorFitForYou, which is my Instagram handle.

Q: I'm excited for you and what you're doing. Thank you so much for all your time. And I look forward to all the stuff we're going to be doing together.
TR: Thank you. I'm excited as well. And thank you so much for this forum and this platform and this space so I can share my voice. I appreciate it.

DR. TEISHA ROBERTSON
www.instagram.com/TaylorFitForYou

As a certified online health and wellness coach, Dr, Teisha Robertson of TaylorFitForYou is passionate about creating a safe and supportive space for busy and overwhelmed women to level up their health through TaylorFit goals, good sleep, nutrition, spirituality, and fitness that can be incorporated into their busy and hectic lives. In the middle of her own health crisis of being pre-hypertensive, Dr. Teisha became committed to focusing on her own health and not becoming a victim of the controllable diseases—high blood pressure, diabetes, high cholesterol, and stroke that currently plague millions of other women across the world.

As a result of her personal journey, Dr. Teisha uses an integrated approach to empowering women by encompassing the mind, body, and soul in her work. She strongly believes that a healthy lifestyle journey is more than working out and is more of an all-inclusive method to achieving, maintaining, and sustaining good health.

Every woman is unique and different in her own right, and Dr. Teisha creates Taylorfit action plans to ensure success. In addition to providing a unique and caring coaching experience to her TaylorFit Queens, she also operates as a motivator, accountability partner, mentor to ensure they achieve their fitness goals.

Holding a Personal Training and Nutrition Coach Certification, Dr. Teisha has collaborated with women on being mindful and intentional about their goals to level up their health. She also uses her Doctorate in Pharmacy Degree to specifically help women on medications caused by their weight and diet to join a community and become healthier to decrease and get off medications. She's spent her time volunteering to present to state agencies, public and private schools, churches and other agencies to spread the word on health and wellness topics ranging from "Sleep, Wake up to Good Health", "Diabetes Awareness and Prevention", and "Healthy Eating Step Up to the Plate", to name a few.

As the founder of TaylorFitForYou, Dr. Teisha brings her wealth of knowledge and background to provide a well-rounded and TaylorFit Online Health Coaching experience for women looking to level up their health.

Speaking positivity into myself, speaking affirmations into me, and just learning to put myself first have helped to get me over many of the obstacles and negativity.

—Dr. Teisha Robertson

DR. DEBORAH HOWELL
Victory in Action
Founder/CEO

CHAPTER 9

Owning Our Health as a Relationship
with Dr. Deborah Howell

HEY THERE, SUPERWOMAN. I AM SO EXCITED today to have my next guest. We were having a little conversation before we started, and she is a veteran and I'm a veteran. I don't get a chance to talk to too many veterans. She was in the Navy and now she has gone on to create an amazing business that we're going to talk about. And I'm also excited because she's going to be my new neighbor. I'm moving into her neighborhood.

Q: Deborah Howell, how are you?
Deborah Howell: I'm wonderful. And I'm excited to meet you and have this conversation.

Q: I am, too. The name of your practice is Victory in Action. And you are a licensed physical therapist, a HeartMath provider, certified trauma-sensitive practitioner, chronic care professional, along with being a health and life coach for healthcare professionals. You're also a best-selling author. Can you tell me how you ended up starting Victory in Action? What brought you to this work?
DH: It was an evolution. When I got out of the Navy, I became a physical therapist. And early on, I was introduced to things I had not expected to find in healthcare, which brought a whole lot of confusion and disappointment but also increased my awareness. Then I ended up getting injured and needing physical therapy and did not receive the kind of care I had expected. Fortunately, at that time I was still new in the game, trying to figure out how I could get back on my feet, and then figure out if I still wanted to do this and how I was going to do it.

Along with my employer job, I was seeing patients privately who were dealing with chronic pain. It was a very, very challenging population to work with while still trying to figure out how not to lose my own health. It didn't work out all that well in the beginning, because there came a point in time, before Victory in Action, that I did have a major health crisis. It wasn't visible—you couldn't look at me and say, "Oh, she's really struggling"—but within me, I could feel the life force was leaving my body. And to know what that feels like is—I never want to feel like that again.

It was a very frightening and uncertain time for me,

because I still had responsibilities. I had responsibilities as a mother, as a wife, and I was still working. As I was trying to deal with my own health, I thought, "How am I going to do all this?"

Victory in Action came out of the words themselves: Victory in Action. Taking action, I knew I had to do something. And being victorious was also meaningful. I wasn't really working with people under the Victory in Action business early on, but I published my first book that way. This book was, *Straight to the Heart of What Matters*. It was a book that spoke to some of the challenges that I had experienced and some of the things that I'd learned as a therapist. And then things sort of evolved and I started learning about the wisdom of the heart—I was coming back into my heart, I was trying not to lose heart, right? Because I think that's what ultimately happened. The disappointment from the system itself, and then the expectations that I had, and adding to it was the ongoing adjustment from a career change after being in the military, which is its own story.

Q: Yes.
DH: But becoming a therapist and getting injured, needing therapy, and all that took place there, I honestly lost heart and did not understand what was taking place. And so, all that led to my own understanding of how to get myself back into my heart and re-approach how I was going to move forward. Ultimately that new approach was to teach what I have learned. So, it's been a process.

Q: It's been a process. It usually is, isn't it? How long were you in the Navy?
DH: I was in for nine years.

Q: Did you get hurt while you were serving in the Navy or was it afterward?
DH: Afterward.

Q: And when you got hurt were you feeling disappointed in your body, the system, the military, the healthcare system?
DH: So, I had a whiplash. That was my original injury. And then I had a fall. As a result, I needed physical therapy and I was receiving therapy. There came a point when I thought, "Wow. I'm a therapist and I am not getting the care that I need. I am not getting better. I am getting worse." It was my own profession. I really felt let down. I did not expect what I had experienced.

And then there is the healthcare system, which relies on band-aids, taking a pill for this or that, and not getting to the underlying root cause of illness. There's a problem with having sufficient time to care and sensitivity in caring. I know that we are taught in school how to work with the body holistically. But a lot of times, because the healthcare system is driven by insurance, it has taken away the autonomy in how we practice and unfortunately, we need the numbers and the reimbursement to make ends meet. That can result in compromising quality of care.

Q: I think it's not just in physical therapy, it's in a lot of areas. I have talked to many doctors and people who opened up their practices, and now a lot of doctors are starting to do non-insurance care where I pay cash, and adding coaching to their practices and doing more consulting. They're just doing different things that would be a little more nontraditional than when they were taught for the same reasons. It's showing up in every part of the system.

DH: Yes, absolutely. The understanding that I came to, which truly led me to the heart of things, was the discouragement that I felt, the emotional distress because I was in pain, I was in constant pain, and no one had time to address my pain. And then finding that the system wanted to send me to a surgeon. That was their priority. That was not my priority. Surgery was not my priority. So, I needed to do my own work to find someone who would take time to work with me. Because I had knowledge of what I thought I needed, and I just needed someone to take time with me, a therapist to take time with me and work with me.

Fortunately, I was able to find a wonderful physical therapist who really cared and took time with me. I was able to get myself back on track, but the level of stress and distress took a toll in another way. It wasn't just a physical injury, it was this internal wear and tear on my nervous system. I was still working with patients that had complications that were ongoing, that were long standing. And again, because time to care is an issue, I was still trying to take whatever time I had to give all that I could. And it was depleting.

And so, knowing that this level of distress does have cumulative effects on the body, and from my own steps to recover, that's the path that I've been wanting to teach others. What do we do when we don't feel supported? What do we do when we don't feel understood, or no one has the time to care? Ultimately, it's my body, and I'm in it 24/7, right? The onus is on me first to understand where I am and take responsibility back. And that's what I had to do. I was upset and knew that was getting in the way of my healing. There was an element of resistance. I was angry, I was hurt, and all of that was a barrier to my recovery in the beginning. I had to learn to let things go. I had to take ownership of my recovery.

Q: Take the responsibility back. What I'm hearing is you were disheartened, heartbroken, all these things, because you care deeply about what you do and now you were experiencing it from the patient side and realizing that it was not working, it was broken. And you had two choices, you could either sit down and ignore it or do something about it. And you did. You decided, "You know what? This is not working, and I'm not going to continue to go down that road. I'm going to make some changes." Which is really what a boss lady does. You make some changes and try to help lead other people into that change, which sounds like what Victory in Action is. What are some other struggles that you've had to go through or hurdles that you had to overcome in your business?

DH: Well, it's still a process to this day. Speaking of boss ladies, my best friend of 30 years was a true boss lady, and her sudden passing profoundly impacted my life. She was a healthcare professional, veteran, and wonderful mom! The experience and conditions around her situation are a big part of my WHY behind the decision to work with healthcare professionals.

It's all been evolving. My personal business has been a small piece, because I am still primarily an employee working in an inpatient rehab. I get to see and experience and help facilitate some deeply transformative experiences that at times feel more like a ministry. Being in the right place at the right time. Being present to who I am caring for. Caring for the whole person. Talking about presence, that's the teaching that I'm bringing forth. It's about being in the heart, being in this caring and compassionate space that is expansive, that enhances our sensitivity and awareness, and our ability to authentically connect.

So, we meet heart to heart, and we meet with a level of understanding that I'm here to care for you. And that understanding comes without me saying anything. It comes with me walking in the room and someone can feel that I'm there, I'm present. I'm not down the hallway or off somewhere in my mind. You know, these things are palpable. So, from an energetic point of view, it's being aware of what's going on in us, that we're present to our own emotion, our own triggers, and things like that because trauma comes along for the ride.

And so, I listen to folks. It's important that we validate where people are and recognize that perspective matters, that someone's perspective on their situation makes it so for them. We come to a place where we honor who we're present to, but we keep sight of where we are as well. There is this relationship, there is an exchange going on.

Being in the heart, the heart has its own intelligence. And it is phenomenal what can take place, in this open space, beyond what is typical in outcomes. Inspiration came to me as an understanding of what starts to move when we are in our heart sincerely to care. And this is where the beauty unfolds.

Q: You would feel like that would be the exact place that a caregiver would be in the heart but the system's not set up that way.
DH: Agreed, however, it is up to the individual practitioner to take notice and take care of themselves from a preventive point of view. Honestly, even when we are in the heart to care, there's something called overcare, compassion fatigue, or vicarious trauma that affects frontline professionals. The experiences we take on, we don't even realize that we're taking in as well. We are energy, right? We're a fluid body, we're an energy body. And so, we are in this energy exchange all the time.

One of the things we must learn as practitioners is how to have healthy boundaries. And when we're in the midst of providing care, we have to learn not to put ourselves on the back burner, which is what I did. And then I was upset with the system and everything. But the key really is to take ownership for our wellbeing. To know our own limits and to ask for help. To show up, and when we show up in this way, it changes the conditions in that environment—the actual conditions that allow for growth and for what can evolve versus creating a barrier. It comes through the heart.

Q: Beautiful. What would you say to a woman who is really looking to have success in her business or in her life? What is the first thing that she should consider?
DH: Know that it's a journey. It's a journey, it's a process. It's taken me quite a while, from 2005. I had a vision back then and it's only beginning right now, so that's a long time. Weathering that, staying with it little by little, and being willing to grow and invest in myself. I had to come into my own relationship with money and something that felt bigger than me. I had to grow into this.

I'm still growing into it and learning to ask for help, because I'm independent and I wasn't one to ask for help. I thought, "I'll figure it out. I'll just do this." Ultimately, I'm learning that it's OK to ask for help. It's not a weakness. It's not going to take anything away. It's learning to use my voice. It's a beautiful process that doesn't always feel so good and warm and fuzzy but it's meaningful.

Q: I love it. What keeps you motivated? What keeps you inspired?
DH: I have four daughters and I look at all my girls and each of them are bits and pieces of me. Some of them are outwardly present and then other parts are more reserved, so I'm seeing myself at different stages in life, through my four daughters. They inspire me to be more. As I want them to live their life fully and to their greatest potential, to do what's in their heart while they're in this life, I want the same for myself. So, my kids inspire me, and my patients inspire me. I have patients saying some of the kindest things to me and I just am so humbled and so grateful and honored to be at a point in their lives to be of service. And I'm very grateful for my life. I know that there's more for me to step into, as I say yes to each moment that unfolds. It's a day-by-day thing.

Q: Do you work with people virtually as well as in an office?
DH: It's kind of a hybrid right now because I am still involved with patient care, but my next steps are with healthcare providers. And so, with all this going on with COVID and all the variants, I'm kind of taking it as it comes. And so, most of my work for healthcare providers is online.

Q: What is the best way for people to connect with you?
DH: My website is VictoryinAction.com and then I've just started a global community of healthcare professionals as part of that, the selfcarechamber.com. I want to support our providers and frontline professionals, because it is a rigorous and demanding profession. It is more challenging than ever.

Q: It definitely is.
DH: We have to take full ownership of our health. This is a deeply personal relationship. Everything in life is relational. And when we step into that space to serve another, who is really needing us to be present and to be well and to offer guidance and constructive support, it's necessary for us to do our self-care work. Trust is lacking in our system. Trust and transparency are lacking. I can tell you that I have come back with a whole different approach that has allowed me to know where I'm focused and to help me to still really enjoy my work. I'm going on almost 30 years in practice.

Q: Well, Dr. Deborah Howell, thank you for sharing your story. I am so excited to have you as a part of this project that we're working on.
DH: Yes. I'm excited as well and for your move to Vegas too.

Q: I am too.

DR. DEBORAH HOWELL

www.VictoryinAction.com

Dr. Deborah Howell is the Founder and CEO of Victory in Action LLC, specializing in Heart-Focused Leadership and Empowerment, and Emotional Resiliency training. She is a Licensed Physical Therapist, HeartMath® Provider, Certified Trauma-Sensitive Practitioner, Chronic Care Professional Health Coach and Life Coach, Best-Selling Author, and Navy Veteran.

Dr. Howell's Signature training, Emotional Muscle Fitness®, is Rehab for the Heart...a practical, experiential, and integrative methodology that enhances the ability to effectively manage stress, cope with change, and build emotional capacity and resilience into everyday life.

Dr. Howell approaches three decades in Clinical Rehabilitative Therapy practice, extensively with oncology, neurological, orthopedic, and trauma involved populations, helping patients navigate through complex and life-altering situations to restore their health, function, hope, and livelihood. Dr. Howell has facilitated deeply transformative experiences for her patients and clients. As a result of professional studies and training and personal application of integrative and mindfulness practices, she offers a breadth of knowledge, experience, and effective evidenced based practices through deeply supportive and trauma-sensitive services to the professional healthcare community as a medical life and health advisor, coach-mentor, educator, and facilitator. Her guidance and programs help healthcare professionals and leaders recharge, renew, and restore a sense of well-being and life purpose.

Inspiration came to me as an understanding of what starts to move when we are in our hearts sincerely to care.

—*Dr. Deborah Howell*

> You can still build a business, have a purpose and work toward that purpose no matter what age you are.
>
> —*Sue Bellion*

SUE BELLION
Sue Bellion
Wellness & Transformational Coach

CHAPTER 10

Don't Give Up Until You Find Your Purpose
with Sue Bellion

HEY THERE, SUPERWOMEN. I AM SO EXCITED TO have my next guest. We were talking about her journey as a wellness and transformational coach, and it's very similar to what I did for about 10 years, working with people who wanted to focus on a healthier lifestyle. I had lost weight and I started feeling amazing and changed my life and I was so inspired by my own transformation that I started working with some other people. So it's really an honor to talk to my next guest, who has gone through a similar transformation and is trying to help other men and women do the same.

Q: Sue Bellion, how are you?
Sue Bellion: I'm doing great today. I'm so happy to have this opportunity to share what I love doing.

Q: What inspired you to start your business?
SB: I've always had an interest in having my own business and I have had many different entrepreneurial side gigs over the years. I always felt like I was looking for a purpose, to have significance and to help people. I went through a few different businesses and learned a lot. I was somewhat successful in most of them but with my current business I've really found where I want to be. I've found what I can identify with and where my strengths are best used, and that's wellness and transformational coaching.

It started with me deciding I needed to improve my health and get well in a lot of ways and I found a plan that I was super successful with. I'm still on my own health journey. There was an opportunity to be a coach for that plan and program and I just got really excited about being able to share that with other people and help them do the same thing that I've done and to join me on that journey.

Q: You found yourself this new lifestyle and you wanted to create things for other people. You really have a desire for helping people to live a fuller life, a life of wellness. You mentioned that you'd tried a few other side gigs first. I know a lot of people are looking for something that will work for them. What is the most important thing to know about finding a business that you can sink your teeth into or build?
SB: You have to believe in what it is that you're promoting, and if it's the type of business where you have to either go through a transformation or improve your health or use a

product, then you have to experience it yourself. I believe you have to have personal experience with it to not only talk the talk but walk the walk.

For me, it was important to personally experience the program and it pressed all the right buttons when I found the specific plan that I'm doing and the community of like minded people that I work with. It's more than just improving your physical health and losing weight. It involves wellness in terms of mind, body, spirit—and ultimately finances, because of the opportunity there is to create a business that can reward you very nicely over time.

Q: What are some hurdles you have overcome, in life or in business, and what did you learn from them?
SB: I think one of the hurdles professionally was in previous businesses when I was not reaching the level of success that I wanted to. It was a challenge then not to lose faith in my ability to find a purpose and a business that works for me, that resonates with me, and that people will identify with. On the personal side, my most difficult challenge was when my husband passed away almost four years ago, in November of 2018. That changed my life drastically—understandably so as I was dealing with the loss and grief. But then it became even more important to me to find a purpose, because I felt like I had lost a lot of my purpose.

Q: Yes.
SB: So, it was finding not only a business purpose, but a personal purpose. What do I do with my life now? That's where I was coming from. It was important to find something that really was important to me and worthwhile, because I knew that any journey, whether a health, wellness, or business

journey, takes a lot of dedication and a lot of focus and I wanted to find that. When my husband passed away four years ago, I was 62 and thinking, OK, I need to work at something, find something that not only is important to me, but that I can be very successful with. I was not looking at it as just something to do until I "retired." I want to do this for the rest of my life. So, I wanted to find something that would be, quite honestly, worthy of my time and my effort.

Q: I love that. I think it's really important that you show this and I'm glad you have the energy for it. Because not everyone has the energy to put in.
SB: Sometimes I wonder where I get the energy! But getting healthy and getting my personal health in order made a tremendous difference. That's so critical for anything, not just for my journey, for my work, for having this business, but for everything. There is a health crisis in this country and it's affecting people in so many different ways, but one of them is that people don't have the energy to do the things they want to, the energy to live the lives they want. That's also something that attracted me to this work—not only for my personal journey, but how universal it is.

Q: Very true. And you can inspire so many people when they see what you're able to do and what you're still doing. Getting and staying healthy as we age is important. It doesn't matter what age you are, you can get healthy.
SB: Yes, I really saw the need and wanted to show people—and women, especially—that age doesn't matter. You can still get healthy, build a business, have a purpose, and work toward that purpose no matter what age you are. I know some people at my age are winding down but , "I'm winding up!"

Q: That's right. What advice would you give another woman who wants to "wind up," who wants to get out there and do something cool and do something new? What would you tell her?

SB: Don't give up, just keep on looking! If you haven't found what really is important to you, what rings your bell—I know that's sort of corny, but something that really works for you, that you can believe in and that you can identify with, keep on looking for that and don't give up. It doesn't matter if you have to try a couple different things until you find something that works for you.

And look for a community of people to work with that will support you regardless of your age, your gender, whatever, because it shouldn't matter. The biggest thing is to not give up. Just keep on doing it, keep on looking for what works for you, and don't get discouraged. Because as we know, anything worthwhile usually doesn't come easy.

Q: That's right. How do you stay motivated?

SB: I love what I do. I love working with people. I coach people in their wellness journey and their transformational journey and I get excited when they have successes. We have a strong culture of celebrating in our community, of celebrating successes. And I love celebrating those successes with people and helping them to realize those successes.

Also encouraging them to pay it forward because that's so much of what we do. If you're having success, then to a certain extent I believe, for myself, there's an obligation to pay it forward. And that's what we encourage people to do and we create that culture of paying it forward, helping other people to achieve the same level of success or any level of success.

Everyone has their own definition of success. Mine is not going to be the same as anyone else's, but we have a community and a culture that respects and honors any success that someone has, whatever level it is. For some people, doing what I'm doing may be so out of their realm of possibility at this time, but by the same token there are people who have more success in doing what I'm doing and I'm a little overwhelmed at the thought of getting to that level. It's a process. You learn as you go and you grow into it. But the biggest thing I would say is don't give up. There are a lot of people who will try to discourage you and say, "What are you doing? Why are you doing that?" If you have a dream and a goal, don't give up.

Q: Is there anything else that you would like to share with my audience about your health and wellness journey? Or the transformation that you've gone through?
SB: You asked about hurdles, and I mentioned the passing of my husband. For me personally, a huge aspect of that was finding strength through my faith, through my family, and through friends. That was huge. The spiritual, faith, whatever you want to call it, everybody has a different definition or a different thing that they potentially would rely on or turn to. For me, my faith was very important.

Also, surround yourself with positive people. I'm also a big believer in self-development, in reading self-development books, and positive books. I'm a big affirmations person. I have them on my phone, I have them at different places, and I say them out loud, because I believe that what you say to yourself, your subconscious believes to be true and will work to make it happen for you. You'll notice more and different things around you. It's all part of your reticular activating system, where you'll have a different level of awareness of opportunities around you. I'm a firm believer in what you feed your mind makes a huge difference in your life.

Q: I love that. Sue, where can people connect with you?
SB: I have a website, suebellion.com. I am in the process of building that and expanding my social media reach. I'm on Facebook and Instagram. I'm working on developing and building my brand and presence on those platforms.

Q: It's been a pleasure talking with you today. I'm excited for all the things that we're doing this year as well so thank you so much.
SB: I enjoyed talking with you too. And I look forward to continuing to share my health journey and paying it forward.

Disclaimer: OPTAVIA makes no guarantee of financial success. Success with OPTAVIA results from successful sales efforts, which require hard work, diligence, skill, persistence, competence, and leadership. Please see the OPTAVIA Income Disclosure Statement (bit.ly/idsOPTAVIA) for statistics on actual earnings of Coaches.

SUE BELLION

Having worked at different entrepreneurial businesses for many years, Sue has found that becoming a wellness and transformational coach to be the most fulfilling and satisfying. After her husband passed away, it was important to Sue to not only work on improving her own health but to find a new purpose and being able to help people transform their health was the perfect way to pay it forward as well. Sue loves working with people of all ages, but hopes to inspire everyone, especially women, that it doesn't matter what your age and that it's not too late to regain or improve your health and to even build a successful business. In addition to her coaching business, Sue is active in her church and looks forward to more golf, hiking and travel in her future. Sue especially enjoys beach vacations and is a big believer in self-care to rejuvenate the body, mind, and spirit.

KAREN RUBINSTEIN
HOW Now Coffee & Community House
Proprietor and Entrepreneur

CHAPTER 11

Don't Give Up till the Miracle Happens
with Karen Rubinstein

HEY THERE, SUPERWOMEN. I AM SO EXCITED FOR my next guest. I met her a couple of weeks ago at an event, and she was telling me about her amazing vision for a coffee shop and community recovery program. She has big dreams and an incredible personal story. I'm looking forward to giving her this space to share all of it and talk about the path she is now on.

Q: Karen Rubinstein, how are you?
Karen Rubinstein: Hi, I'm great, Tam. Thanks for having me.

Q: The name of your coffee shop is How Now Coffee & Community House. There is so much to talk about here but let's start with: Why coffee?
KR: Well, Tam, as an alcoholic who goes to a 12-Step meeting every day, coffee is very important!

Q: So funny. That makes sense, actually! Let's talk about your vision for How Now Coffee & Community House and how you see it growing into a place of refuge for people.
KR: Long story short, my husband and I—he's very supportive—were thinking of opening a halfway house, a sober living house. But there's a lot that goes with a project like that, there's a tough side to it, overdoses, and other issues. But the focus of the sober living house—I kept waking up every morning last summer, thinking, "We could have 12-Step meetings at the house, we could do meditation, we could do yoga." My friend is a chef, and she has a culinary school so I was thinking that she could teach healthy eating. Everything would be about health, mind, and spirit.

One of the next things we thought about is that we live near a town that doesn't really have a coffee house. And I thought let's do a coffee house and keep the aspects that I really loved about having a sober living house. I'm very community minded, connected with the Rotary and Chamber of Commerce, I've always been community minded. I love bringing people together. I also get a lot of questions, like,

"How did you become an alcoholic? I don't understand." So, it's education for the public, it's destigmatizing, because, you know, if there are six million alcoholics in this country and each of them has 30 close friends and relatives, well, that's a lot more than six million people who are affected by addiction.

So, I added "Community House" because I wanted to be inclusive. It's not just for people in recovery, although that is the focus. When I got out of rehab two years ago, I realized there are not too many places for people to go to get support and to have a nice time and gather, outside of 12-Step meetings. So, it's going to be a fun spot. We're trying to do a country chic type of look, something really comfortable and homey, so that when you go in, you just want to stay.

We're going to get beat-up leather couches, my cousin recommended getting a little electric fireplace, we'll have literature there—brochures and materials from different rehab facilities, a lot of information that people can grab. We'll also have a library and a little bookshop that will include some positive upbeat books offering hope and education.

We'll also have activities such as yoga, meditation and crafts on different nights. There are a lot of people who are homeless, who are in addiction or alcoholics, so on craft nights we'll make handcrafted knit caps and stuff for them. I also know a couple of people in recovery who have bands, so on Friday and Saturday we'll have live music, just to have fun, relax, and bring people together. That's the whole goal.

Q: I love that. Tell me a little more about your background, your alcoholism and what led you to recovery.
KR: Well, they say that you're an alcoholic before you ever know it, and I really thought I was an alcoholic for the past

15 years or so, but it started before that. How you were raised doesn't really matter. You could have a good family, a bad family, or an unsupportive family. I happened to have a very turbulent background, where we weren't allowed to express ourselves or have emotions. There was a lot of yelling. So, I learned to be perfect, keep my head down, and just stuff everything down inside. When I went away to college, that was my first release in life, you know? I jumped into it. I joined every club, I was very active, and I also drank a lot.

But I thought everybody was doing it. Drinking made me feel normal. It made me feel relaxed around people. I was the party girl. I assumed that was going to end when I graduated, but I continued partying and clubbing in the city throughout my twenties. Then I got married—and I'll tell you, there's a lot of drinking in the suburbs. A lot of hidden Baileys and liquor in the coffee cups people are sipping from at town events. The book clubs that I joined were just excuses to drink wine, nobody read the book.

So, it continued, but I still thought drinking was normal. Then I went through a trauma, and the way that I dealt with it was to just check out and dive into a bottle. I didn't want to face anything. I didn't want to feel anything. I thought that was how you coped. I always grew up with, "Oh, you're stressed out, here's a glass of wine." I turned to drinking a lot of wine. We'd buy it by the box. Because I'm thrifty, let's buy a box, you know?

And I always thought, when I'm not in any pain, I'll stop. This is temporary. So, we moved back to New Jersey, and I'm like, "OK, I'm in a good place, I've got a job locally, I like the people I work with, I have friends, I'm going to stop." But I couldn't. I just couldn't. The craving was too horrible. Physically, when I tried to stop, I had night terrors and trembling. I tried stopping several times and I kind of skirted around the 12-Step Program, but I didn't understand alcoholism and addiction.

Finally, it got so bad when Covid hit and I was really isolated at home with my husband, that enough was enough. I felt physically ill all the time. I told my husband that for my own safety, I had to go to detox. So, I checked myself in and they recommended treatment and I'm so glad they did. I went out to Bucks County, Pennsylvania, where they have a 90-day IOP, intensive outpatient program. They introduced me to the 12-Steps. That is the base of their program.

After a couple of weeks of 12-Step Zoom meetings, I looked at the people on the screen and thought, "Oh, my God, they're telling my story. I relate to these people." I was learning so much, and I looked at how happy they were and how together, and I thought "This is what I want. How do I get it?" So, I got a sponsor, like they suggested, I did anything anybody asked to get sober.

That also leads me back to the name of the café, "H.O.W. Now." It's a little wink, wink to people in recovery. H.O.W. stands for Honest, Open, and Willing, which is the foundation for anybody to stay in recovery, to stay sober. I had to be honest with myself in many ways, not just about being an alcoholic, but about really taking a good look at myself. I had to be open to suggestions, and I had to be willing to do the work.

Q: That is a powerful story. How do you continue to stay motivated and inspired?

KR: That's a good question. I feel motivated every morning. I feel blessed. I feel very alive and grateful. I'm grateful I'm sober. I'm grateful for my life. As for inspiration, I wake up every morning with good thoughts and I say a prayer and I do a meditation every day, and the thoughts really flood in. The inspiration is that I feel like my purpose is to help people. I can't save the world, but I can do a little cultivating of my own garden. I can help people in my backyard. So, every single day, I do something that moves us toward opening the café.

For example, I'm making little catnip bags and those are very special to me. My friend Kat (Kathryn) overdosed and died a year ago, on the night of my one-year sober anniversary. Kat was such a lovely woman. We lived in the same sober living house in rehab. She has a young daughter who was Kat's world, of course. Kat always wanted her to go to better schools. They're from an area of D.C. without good schools. So, I named the "Katnip " with a K, for Kat, and all proceeds from those items—Katnip tea, Katnip bags, and everything—all that is specifically for her daughter's education. But we'll have other items for sale at the shop too, like homewares, T-shirts, and baseball caps.

Q: That's amazing. You're getting inspired by being able to help other people. What advice would you give to someone else who is struggling through recovery and really trying to make it and come out on the other side?
KR: I see it happen all the time. Part of being in a 12-Step Program is service to others in need. Once you get yourself whole and you're spiritually sound, you reach out to help others. So, when I see people struggling, and it's not uncommon, I tell them not to isolate. Reach out for help and don't turn down any help. Isolation is a biggie. So,

the fellowship is there, really, for support. Because who knows alcoholism better than an alcoholic? You really can't tell these things to "normies", as we call them. You risk being judged.

The other thing is that you have to do the work. And that involves doing the 12-Steps. I actually was working on my fourth step today, which is really amazing. You put down all your resentments to anybody you've had resentment toward since you've been alive. And believe it or not, I have like 204 people. And my husband was like, "Oh, my God. Are you an angry person?" And I'm like, no, if you really sat down and thought about it you can have lots of small resentments—I mean, some of them are goofy, like a friend broke my Snoopy doll in kindergarten. I've gotten over it, but that was a big resentment for a little girl. So, you assess your entire life. Basically, what you're doing is trying to see a pattern, because there's something that is continuing throughout your life. You find it's the same resentment over and over.

The 12-Step program promises that before you're halfway through the work, you'll be amazed. I've been amazed a million times over. I never thought I would be in this situation. Thank you again for inviting me to be in this book. It's like the possibilities are endless. Another major thing to tell people who are struggling is: Don't give up till the miracle happens. Hang in there, go to the meetings. If you have to, I suggest doubling up on meetings. Reach out, reach out, reach out. We're there for you.

Q: I love that. Don't give up until a miracle happens. That's the truth. I think you can probably take that on just in general. That's such a good one.
KR: Thanks. I didn't coin it. That's another 12-Step phrase. We have a lot of slogans. But they're really helpful. They stick with you, you know?

Q: They do stick with you. During Covid, a lot of people were struggling. Alcohol use was increasing, people were trying to cope with challenges to their mental health. It was a lot. But you got help. What made you do that? A lot of people just kept struggling. What made you say, "Enough is enough"?
KR: My rock bottom was the day that I couldn't sit still from the anxiety I was feeling. I was jumping out of my skin and my mind was racing. Like I said, I wasn't feeling physically well, so I was worried for my health. But once I started to worry about my mental health, I thought, "I can't lose my mind." I basically hit a dead end.

There is a liquor store near where I worked, and during the Covid pandemic the owner of the store said he was alarmed by the increase in sales. He wasn't happy about the drastic increase in sales, he was alarmed!

Again, drinking is a societal norm. If you want to relax, if you're stressed out, you're conditioned to have a glass of wine or something. That's pretty typical. And I think some people don't realize that they're using it as a crutch instead of dealing with their emotions. They can't help it. But they might be like me in that they were thinking, "It's just during Covid, and then I'll stop." They don't realize that once you get addicted—well, here's another expression: Once you're a pickle, you can't go back to being a cucumber. Once you cross that line into addiction, you can't go back. I know I can never have a drink again. Ever.

Q: **Wow, you are so inspiring. Thank you for sharing your wisdom and your process. I know it's every day and it's one day at a time but thank you so much for being that example for all of us. Tell us where we can find out a little more about you, about the coffee shop, and how we can support your efforts.**
KR: Absolutely. Thanks, Tam, and I've really enjoyed this conversation. We do have a website that I designed, which is www.hownowcoffee.com, and our email is hownowcch@gmail.com. And then 908-723-7322 is the phone number.

Q: **Thank you, Karen. I cannot wait for all the amazing things that we'll be doing this year.**
KR: I know! And my husband's so excited. Thank you again and stay tuned, Tam.

KAREN RUBINSTEIN

Karen Rubinstein has more than two years of sobriety and had many years lost as an active alcoholic.

Growing up in New Jersey, within view of Manhattan, she dreamt of a life beyond suburbia with no idea what that was or how to attain it. She often said, "I felt everyone had a guidebook to life except me."

Drinking helped her find her escape but eventually she hit "rock bottom" – frightened she was losing her mind, her health and even her soul. In 2020 she told her husband she had to go to detox, or she'd die.

After almost five months in rehab, Karen was introduced to the 12 Step program and finally found the coping skills she needed to live.

Karen lives with her husband of 32 years, her dog and two cats. Active in the 12 Steps, she's working on opening a recovery-based coffee house.

She now has her guidebook of life and is happy, joyous, and free.

Promise that before you're halfway through the work, you'll be amazed. Don't give up till the miracle happens.

—Karen Rubinstein

SECTION 3

Business

KRISTEN KRAMER
Bold Moves Boss
Business Coach-Consultant

CHAPTER 12

Doing Things Your Way to Ignite the Spark Inside You
with Kristen Kramer

HEY THERE, SUPERWOMEN. I AM SO EXCITED about this conversation. Women Who Boss Up started a few years ago when we began reaching out to women who were launching businesses, writing books, changing careers, and doing many amazing things. And we also started doing meet-and-greets. Well, lo and behold, I have met some of the most incredible women in my meet-and-greets. Including Kristen Kramer. She had the energy that I love. She had the boldness that I love. She made me laugh right away. We ended up talking and realizing we also had a lot in common. And now she has just shifted her successful business into a compelling new direction with a new name: Bold Moves Boss. So I'm excited to have her here.

Q: Kristen Kramer, how are you?
Kristen Kramer: I'm doing fantastic, Tam. I so appreciate being part of this and having a chance to share my story with you and your listeners and folks that'll be reading this later. Before we even get started, I really want to thank you for the community that you've built, because I did meet you through the meet-and-greet and I love going to those. And it's given me an amazing opportunity to connect with other women business owners who are blazing their own trail and creating the future that they want instead of sitting and waiting for other people to create it for them. They're really making bold moves like a bold moves boss to step into their own power.

When I started my business in 2011, it was born out of being painted into a corner. I was either going to get another job in the hotel industry, or I was gonna have to figure out something else to do. So, I launched my business as a virtual assistant and very quickly the business began to grow, which is great. It was a very good thing. I didn't have to spend a lot of time in heavy prospecting, which was nice. No cold calling—sweet. But over the years, it morphed into and evolved into a business management service. And now this next evolution of the company is Bold Moves Boss.

I am taking all of the experience that I've gained over the years in scaling my own business several times over, becoming very familiar with the infrastructure and creating systems and procedures, and being familiar with way more tech than I should be familiar with, probably, and folding that into Bold Moves Boss. I want to take all of those years of experience and help other women entrepreneurs avoid the pitfalls that I went through in scaling my business, in building a team, and in trying to figure out how to do everything. How do you build a business?

And one of the most important things is how to get past the fear of success. When you start out, maybe you feel overwhelmed, and your thought process is "I already feel overwhelmed and I'm already struggling to manage the one or two or five clients that I have—or maybe no clients at the very beginning—what's it gonna be like when I have 10 clients or 20 clients or more?" And so my theory is that a lot of us get stuck in that place and it's not a fear of failure. It's really a fear of your business taking off like a runaway train and you're not prepared and so you get caught with your pants down, so to speak.

Q: And you feel like you can't handle it, so you just kind of pull yourself back. I've seen this happen from time to time again. I was in that space too. You just keep pulling yourself back. But you can be bold instead, if you boss up, then you'll get over that and you'll take that leap anyway. You say, "I don't know what to do, but let's figure this out."
KK: Yes. And that's exactly the mentality that I had in the first 10 years of my business: Sell it now, figure it out later. Land the sale, figure it out later. When I was in the hotel industry, my operations team used to say that salespeople sell the dream and operations have to service the nightmare. They'll never admit it, but they did say it. And this is very true for an entrepreneur. You know the sayings "never stop selling" or "always be closing." And of course, that

mentality morphs over time because we want to serve at the highest level that we can. So, it's not about just closing deals but taking the client and then celebrating for a split second and all of a sudden that troll in the back of your head starts beating the drum of, "You don't even know how to use that platform." "You have no idea how to launch a program." "You've never done that before." "What were you thinking?"

Q: I'm so glad you're bringing this up. To everyone reading or listening right now, you're going into the crazy, crazy mind of an entrepreneur. One of the things that I really like about you, Kristen, is that you are always learning and adding new ideas to what you already know, and that's how you keep moving forward. The name of your company, Bold Moves Boss, makes so much sense because you are all about making bold moves and learning and adding to where you're going. I love it.

KK: Yes. It really is ever-evolving. I almost picked the new brand name to be something about evolution, but I just couldn't get it to sync up. So Bold Moves Boss is where I landed, but what's funny is I got a lot of pushback on the branding because people said nobody likes a boss. Bosses are dictators or bosses just aren't nice. You want to be a leader. It was funny to me because that suggests that being a boss and being a leader are mutually exclusive, which I don't think they are. If you have a good boss, they're also a good leader.

But the spirit behind Bold Moves Boss is about stepping into your personal power. Being the boss of you. Being the boss of your business. Owning the CEO hat, being the boss of your business, being the boss of your future, and the experience that you want to have in life now. And being the boss of where you're headed, instead of feeling like you're at the mercy of everything and everyone around you. So, it's really about stepping up and bossing up and sort of taking the bull by the horns and taking control of your life and your business and your future and being a trailblazer. I think it's great to be a boss.

Q: I do too. I relate to it personally, because there are certain situations where you want to hide or you feel small, and at those times you need to remember, "No, you can do this. You have to boss up." I think women forget that all the bossing up they do for their kids, for their husbands, for all these different things. Then they think about starting a business and they forget. They think, "I'm too small. I can't do this." You can do this. We didn't know a thing when we had kids, right? We didn't know a thing, but we bossed up. What are some of the difficulties you've experienced, whether in your life or your business?

KK: I think early on it was learning to let go of being in control. And that sounds weird because I just finished telling you to be the boss, right? Be the boss of your business, be the boss of you, your future, everything, and that insinuates clutching control with both hands, white knuckles, like, don't let go. When I started my business, I kept telling myself the myth and the story, "Surely, this will level out eventually and it won't feel like I'm constantly in a hurricane being whipped around." And it took me three years to realize that's a lie that we tell ourselves. And in fact, my justification was that if it ever calms down like that, then something is seriously wrong, and I haven't figured it out yet. Like I'm probably going out of business and just don't know it yet. So, it's never going to level out. It's always going to be chaos. It's functional chaos when you get to a certain point, but it's always chaos. So that, I think, was the biggest lesson I learned early on. The other thing that I learned probably between years five and eight was that done well is better than perfect.

Q: Oh, my goodness. Yes.
KK: Yes. And when I got to that life cycle in my business, I was building a team and I fixated for a long time—they would all agree with this!—on them doing it exactly, to the letter, the way I did it. But what I learned is that my clients didn't notice a difference. They didn't notice a difference between me doing it exactly the way I had always been doing it for years and my team getting it done close enough. One, it taught me that it's okay to let go of some of that control. And the other thing was that I also found that if I just allowed things to sort of unfold naturally, instead of trying to shove a square peg into a round hole constantly, always fighting against the tide to force things to happen, things actually came together really well, and we picked up momentum.

Having a team helped me not be the bottleneck in my business as well. So that was a big change, and it took me a while to get a good team because you go through people who don't have the same level of commitment or they don't have any skin in the game so they're not vested in the overall success of your business sometimes. So, it took a while to get a team that was truly vested and cared about the success of my business because they understood that when the business is successful and we're making our clients successful, then they too will be successful.

That also allowed me to foster a culture in my company

where we worked as a cohesive team. Because they knew that if I put together a procedure and they thought, "It looks nice on paper and I appreciate that you put all this work into it, but the reality does not match up to this," they could come to me and tell me. They could say, "Hey look, this, this is not working, and I think we can do it better, and here's how I think we can do it better." I was always very open to allowing clients and my team to come to me with those ideas so that we could continue building on what we've learned. So, we could always continue to grow and evolve.

Q: So true. How do you stay inspired?
KK: Well, very carefully. One of the challenges that I've faced over the past few years is being in this very bizarre space of feeling inadequate. I'm a type-A personality if you haven't guessed that, and so that's kind of a weird anomaly for me. And of course, with Covid, the last two years have been nothing *but* an anomaly so part of it was just dealing with that. But the experience did help me get back in touch with some of the habits that keep me motivated and help me shift from feeling like I'm not good enough, I'm not adequate enough. I don't want to disappoint people or myself, things like that. Those types of thoughts.

I know it sounds cliché but one of the things that I do is meditate for at least 20 minutes every day. I have to do a guided meditation because there is way too much chatter going on up in my brain for me to just focus on breathing, so I use the Calm app. I set it to ocean waves and I listen to the guided meditation for at least 20 minutes. The other thing that I do that I'm pretty strict about is from the moment I get up, while I'm in the shower, the whole kit and caboodle of getting ready in the morning, I'm playing motivational audio in the background. My family is like, somebody give me earplugs so I don't have to listen to this anymore—like Tony Robbins, Mel Robbins, all of them. Really, all of them. Sometimes I listen to Alan Watts and Ram Das just because they talk about quantum physics. I call it brain food. I have a playlist called "Mind-Bending" and that's where they go.

Q: See, this is why you're growing. This is the thing, I'm telling you. You have to listen to these things whether or not it sounds cliché or obvious or whatever.
KK: To me, it's like, if I'm sitting there in my normal habit, which is trying to placate the inner voice saying, "That's a load of BS, you're never gonna get it done, you're not capable of doing this," then the only thing I'm going to do is feel like shit. Straight up, right?

So, what's the harm in drinking the Kool-Aid from the positivity well? At best, I buy into it and I feel better and I'm motivated and it gets my head straight. It gets me in a better space where I can be creative and create for my business and clients. Worst case, I'm like, "This is such a load of crap, and I can't believe people fall for this." But even if I'm saying that it's still better than thinking I'm not enough. All that's going to do is keep holding me back and making me feel like crap every day. So, I figured, what the hell.

Q: I used to do the same thing a lot. I still do. I'll take a few minutes and watch something or listen to something. I also lately have been listening to Brain FM to get me to condense my day so that I'm not working all day long without getting anything done. So, all these little tips are so, so good. What other advice would you give to a female entrepreneur who is looking to be successful or maybe already has a business and is looking to grow or evolve?

KK: This will sound a little counterintuitive, but I would say stop taking the advice of everybody around you. Stop seeking more advice and do it your way. Just do it your way. Because you can be doing all of the things that everybody tells you you're supposed to do. And I fell into this trap for the last two years. Doing all the things that everybody said I was supposed to do in this new market, new business world, and it wasn't working. I wasn't getting traction. I'm rebuilding my business because I lost 90-plus percent during Covid, so that forced me to evolve into something else. You know, maybe their advice works for them and maybe it works for a lot of other people, but you have to do it your way and you have to do it in a way that is going to ignite that spark deep inside you. That's going to light you up and just set your soul on fire. When you feel that, that is when things will start happening for you.

Q: That's when it happens when you start getting to flow, and you're excited. I love this, Kristen. There are a lot of people that need what you're giving out. How can people connect with you and find out more about Bold Moves Boss?

KK: The website, BoldMovesBoss.com, is the best way to find out more about me. I've got some freebies there too. I'm on LinkedIn under Kristen Kramer as well as on Facebook. And of course, people can always email me at kristen@boldmovesboss.com. Super simple.

Q: Super simple. Kristen, thank you. I'm looking forward to all the amazing stuff that we're up to this year.
KK: Yes. I'm excited. It's 2022. We're going to make it happen.

KRISTEN KRAMER
www.boldmovesboss.com

Kristen Kramer is a Business Coach-Consultant | Co-Author Amazon Best Seller | Bold Moves Boss Up Your Business | F-bomb droppin' Mom | Tell it like it is | Unapologetically Authentic | Success or failure OWN it | Daring to DREAM BIG Bold Moves Boss

For more than 11 years, she has provided business management services to entrepreneurs and business owners; showing them how to double their time, maximize profits, and create a business that serves THEM and the world they wish to serve.

Kristen Kramer is the founder of Bold Moves Boss and best-selling co-author of "Life by Design". Kristen works with business owners who are overwhelmed & frustrated trying to figure out their systems, processes, & tech stack. Her 360 approach crushes overwhelm & shows you the bold moves YOU can take to boss up your profits & love your business again!

She's passionate about making the work you do with your clients more impactful so that every spark she (re)ignites, ignites the spark in others to set the world on fire.

It's okay to let go of some of that control. Stop seeking more advice and just do it your way. Just do it your way.

—Kristen Kramer

MASSIEL MEDINA
Your CFO on the GO
Founder, Business Coach & Mentor

CHAPTER 13

Feeding Our Minds in Different Ways
with Massiel Medina

HEY THERE, SUPERWOMEN. I AM SO EXCITED today to have my next guest. I could say that every single business needs what she does. She is Your CFO On The Go—that is the name of her business—and she is filling such a unique niche. I was actually just thinking, "Does she have openings for new clients?" I literally know people who need what she does. But let's get to it because she has a compelling background that led her into this work and I'm excited to hear about it.

Q: Massiel Medina, how are you?
Massiel Medina: Hello, Tam. Thank you so much for having me. I'm excited to be here.

Q: Tell me about your background. You started a family-owned business, right?
MM: Yes.

Q: My parents had a business too. In your case, you ran the back end for 20+ years, is that right?
MM: Yes. It was the neighborhood supermarket and I started working there as a cashier during the summer when I was in high school. I eventually met my (now former) partner there and we started from the bottom and grew it into a business with 20 locations. I ran the back office for about 20 years. Then in 2014 I left the business and my older son took over what I was doing and stayed in the business with his father.

Q: Very cool. Let's talk about exactly what it is that you do as a CFO. What is the difference between a CFO and a bookkeeper or an accountant? How are they all related?
MM: Everybody gets that confused, because it's all finances, right? A bookkeeper does the day-to-day financial records work in any business. When it comes to a CFO, it's like overseeing what the bookkeeper is doing, what's going on in the business, strategizing, looking at all the numbers. An accountant is different. The accountant wraps up all of that and submits tax forms. They will also do what a CFO does, but they don't do the day-to-day work or the training or the supervision of the bookkeeper. An accountant just reviews the numbers and gives you your P&L, your cash flow. I do

that as well but I also will go into a business and train the bookkeeper to do the day-to-day work.

Q: How do you look at business strategy and ways for people to grow their business? Do you look at trends or ways they can position their business?
MM: I review all their numbers, looking where there could be leaks, where they can improve, what departments need attention. I specialize in the supermarket industry. So, for example, there are different departments within a supermarket, so we want to see how the grocery department is doing, how the meat department is doing, how the deli department is doing. We will go over all of those departments and see where we can work the profits up. We look at pricing. There are different strategies to it, right? So you have to see if the transportation is included in your price or the labor is included in it. It's the whole big picture that you have to look at. And then we'll work through the departments.

Q: I love that you're niched, that you're working in a very specific arena. Is it hard to find supermarkets to work with?
MM: Honestly, not for me because I've been in the industry for such a long time. I'm known in the industry, among all the independent supermarkets in my area where I started. I am really referral-based. Everybody that I get—just a little while ago, I got a call, and I had to tell the person I am booked until September. I can meet you, I can have a conversation with you, but I cannot take you on as a client until then. It's a lot of work to onboard someone and to go through the process. So to your question, I've been very lucky that I'm in the industry where I specialize and I'm an expert. I get everybody by word of mouth.

Q: What prompted you to leave the family business and start your own? What led you to Your CFO On the Go?

MM: When I first left, to be honest, I had no idea what I was going to do. My father got sick, so I took time off to take care of him. And when he passed away, I was like, "All right, what am I going to do in my life?" I didn't want to go back into the supermarket industry. I really said that to myself: "I don't want to go back." I didn't want to do the day-to-day work. It's a lot of work.

Randomly, a few weeks after my father had passed away, I got a call from an accountant I had worked with for years. They reached out and said, "We know you know QuickBooks and we have a client that needs help. Since you're not working, do you mind?" I thought, sure, I enjoy it and it'll keep me busy until I figure out what I'm going to do. Again, I didn't want to go back into the business, both because of the day-to-day work and also because I wanted to do something fun.

In my mind, doing numbers—because it was my own business—was not fun. So I continued to get clients randomly, just like that. I was not promoting myself, I was not putting myself out there. And this lasted for about six years. I thought of it as a hobby. I was keeping myself busy. And then around 2019 I started to get busier and I realized I didn't have structure. I was just helping people out.

At that point, I said to myself, "Okay, the need is there, I love to serve, how can I make this work where it's fun for me as well?" I was serving them, I was helping the business grow, and I was fulfilling myself at the same time. It all goes hand in hand. So I really sat down and started to look at it. I got a business coach who really helped me strategize and just put things together. And then COVID hit, and that gave me even more time to really dig into it.

Then I started working from home with the clients I already had and in November 2020, I officially launched. That is when I really put myself out there for everyone to know that I was actually doing this. That's when I came up with the name as well. In the beginning of 2020, when I started talking to my coach, I actually went on a retreat and I was expressing to everyone what I wanted to do. I was even thinking I might create a course. I was trying to figure it out. And one of the girls at the retreat said to me, "So what is it that you do?" And I explained it to her. She goes, "Oh, you're a CFO on the go." And that really clicked with me!

As I said before, I wanted it to be something fun, something that I enjoyed, and at the same time, I was serving. So that prompted me to sit down and figure it out. I took my time, I did the branding, I worked with my coach, and I launched at the end of 2020.

Q: That is incredible. I love your story, that you found something you love to do and something that really is needed. What are some of the ups and downs you have experienced, whether in life or in business?
MM: I would say one of the harder points for me when I started was thinking, "Who's going to want to hire me?" Even though I was getting people, I knew I was getting them because people were referred to me, right? So I put myself out there a little bit more. I don't have a college degree. I'm not an accountant. Why would people come to me? How would they trust me?

Then I realized that, you know, it wasn't a degree that was going to make me or break me, it was my experience.

I ran an empire of 20 locations and I was doing the day to day work, working very hard, and I put myself in situations to learn and grow. That experience was what made me. But that was one of my biggest obstacles, to be very honest.

Q: Yes, a lot of women go through that, the imposter syndrome. Who am I to do this? Am I good enough? I went through that myself. That is very relatable to a lot of people. What advice would you give another woman starting a business? How could she get going and get past that limiting belief?

MM: The number one thing I would say is it's never too late to begin. I started this business in my mid-forties. It is never too late to start over and to start a business that you're passionate about. What has also helped me along the way is having my support team. Sometimes people think of a support team as a coach and a professional, but it doesn't have to be a coach. Yes, I did have my coach and yes, I had my friends and family that were supporting me, but within your circle, within your tribe, you have those special people that you can go to and have a conversation with and they can give you that positive energy. My friends and family also help me see my strength. And sometimes we—again, because of imposter syndrome—we don't see that. So having those people that inspire you and elevate you, empower you, having that tight circle, that is golden. To me, that's golden.

Q: It is. I love that. What is inspiring you now? What is motivating you now?

MM: The day-to-day routines keep me motivated, feeding my mind in different ways, listening to a podcast, reading a book, listening to an audio book. So many little things just to feed my mind, move my body, connect, have my community. That's essential for me, my network, my close circle, and always talking to others about what I'm going through so they can see the other side and, you know, kind of help me go through that.

Q: What else would you like to share with people about your business or about their business that they should remember? What should people be aware of when they're in business?

MM: One of the main things that I see a lot is that when people start a business, they're not aligned or they don't have their expenses aligned, they're just kind of all over the place. You don't have to use QuickBooks, you could use any software or you could use a spreadsheet. But somewhere you need to put down what's going on, what your income is, what your expenses are—even your little expenses, even if it's just a meal, whatever it is that belongs to your business, track it. Track everything.

You could use a spreadsheet. You could use an app—there are so many free apps out there. But track it so you can know what's going on. In the beginning, yes, there's definitely going to be ups and downs where you're probably not going to have a profit right away, depending on the type of business that it is. You're going to start by getting yourself out there. That's another thing that I say, because that has really, really helped me, even though I was scared. I was very scared in the beginning. But putting yourself in uncomfortable places, putting yourself in rooms where there are big thinkers, people that you can relate to, that are like-minded, they're going to inspire you.

Q: Right. I love that. Where can people find you if they want to know more about your business or your services?
MM: My website is YourCFOOnTheGo.com and they can look me up there. I'm also on Instagram @YourCFOonthego. Those are the two best places.

Q: Massiel, thank you so much for your time today. I look forward to all the stuff we're going to be doing together.
MM: Thank you so much for having me, Tam. I really appreciate it. I had so much fun.

MASSIEL MEDINA
www.yourcfoonthego.com

Massiel Medina is the CEO & Founder of Your CFO on the Go.

She spent 20+ years running the back-end of the family business, where she fell in love with QuickBooks and the way it empowers business owners to make informed and strategic decisions.

Throughout that time, She acquired the experience and skills to run back-office operations, conduct internal reviews, manage and control A/R & A/P, and much more for 20+ food retail locations.

Today, she educates and empowers business owners and their teams by coaching and training them on how to use QuickBooks and SOPs (standard operating procedures) for their business, allowing teams to excel in their careers and giving business owners the confidence in their numbers to grow their business.

> Number one thing I would say is it's never too late to begin.
>
> —Massiel Medina

AMANDA MA
Innovate Marketing Group
Founder & CEO

CHAPTER 14

Taking the Leap of Calculated Faith
with Amanda Ma

HEY THERE, SUPERWOMEN. I'M SO EXCITED TODAY to have my next guest. I love marketing, went to college for marketing, and have been working in marketing in some capacity for many years. So I know this is going to be a really fun conversation. Mrs. Amanda Ma is CEO of Innovate Marketing Group, which specializes in event management, which can be a critical piece of an overall marketing strategy. And it is not easy, so let's get into it.

Q: Amanda Ma, how are you?
Amanda Ma: Good. Thanks for having me here.

Q: It's so good having you. Tell me a little bit about yourself. Are you originally from Los Angeles?
AM: I was born in Taipei, Taiwan and I moved here with my parents when I was 10 years old. Our family moved here in pursuit of the American Dream. We had to adapt to a new environment, new language, new everything. It was exciting yet unfamiliar at first.

Q: When did your interest in business develop?
AM: I always knew I wanted to be an entrepreneur because my dad was an entrepreneur. I knew I was interested in business. But as to what type of business, I did not know. I even went to school for business and something about business just always fascinated me.

Q: My parents were both entrepreneurs as well. I think that is a benefit that we get a chance to see them struggle and see them work through stuff. What really inspired you to actually start your own business? Was it your dad and watching him?
AM: Oh, yes. I grew up in the showroom. My dad was in the patio umbrella business. So, my cousin and I would go into the showroom... We would just go there and play and watch my dad in action. He also flew around a lot for the business, but despite that, he was always there for us. In my memory, he was such a hustler, such a fantastic entrepreneur, and an even better Dad. I thought to myself, "I want to be like him when I grow up."

Q: That's exactly how I felt when I watched my parents. I'm like, "How did they know to do this?" Because my parents did not go to college. I just watched them hustle and just get out there. When Covid came around, I thought back to what my parents did and that really drove me. I was like, "Oh, my parents had it way more difficult than I ever did. So, let's get it going." Did you kind of feel like that too?
AM: Oh, my gosh, yes. So many feelings during the pandemic. You take everything with a grain of salt, and you just embrace what's happening and do your very best. At first it was very challenging but after a mindset shift, we got to work. When there is a will, there is a way.

Q: How long have you been in business now?
AM: I've been in business for 16 years now. All in the event management space.

Q: What are some of the most fun or successful events you've done?
AM: There are so many! One highlight would definitely be when TikTok launched its headquarter office in Los Angeles. They're one of our clients and we did their grand opening party, and it was epic. Another one that really stood out was for our client, The Latino Coalition. A vital part of that event involved working with the White House and Secret Service because the President of the United States was one of the high-profile speakers among many others. After planning a very successful event dealing with the White House and Secret Service, we elevated our experience and portfolio a thousand-fold. It was very memorable, I'll just put it that way, both in lack of sleep and lots of preparation, but also the level of detail and

being able to problem-solve and think on the spot. Our team had to do that, and they did an absolutely fantastic job. It was remarkable the following day to see our event on the front page of the newspaper. We love helping fuel brands to elevate their event experiences.

Q: That's part of the skills you need for marketing and in particular for events. You've got to be able to think on your feet. You've got to improvise and make it work. I can't even imagine all of that, which is normal pressure, and then adding the pressure of the White House, the Secret Service, and all that.
AM: Yes. Working with The White House and Secret Service is indeed an art. Highly complex logistics when it involves The President of The United States. From the safety path, green room, song preference, press stands to many others. Staying calm under pressure is essential.

Q: I love it. What are some challenges or obstacles you have faced, whether in life or business? Entrepreneurship is not easy.
AM: Entrepreneurs are definitely a different breed, a very special breed. Because we are the type of people that say, "We can make this happen" or "We can do it better." Owning your own business is like riding a roller coaster. The high moments are incredible, and the low moments are sometimes insanely painful. But each time we pick ourselves up again and back in for the fight to do it better and smarter.

Two significant challenges stood out in my entrepreneur journey, the first event planning agency that I co-founded, I originally had a business partner, but after eight years, our visions diverged and so we decided to go our separate ways.

You would think that's pretty easy, but it was very challenging to separate. We actually ended up going through a business dissolution and that is a big process. I hope anyone that's listening would never go through that. It was one of the lowest points in my life. And I felt so lonely and discouraged about why I even became an entrepreneur. Then again, a lot of my entrepreneur friends would tell me, "Oh, now you've been initiated. Welcome to the club." Right? I just call it a very expensive lesson. And ultimately, now, I'm an even better entrepreneur for it.

After that, I started Innovate Marketing Group, focusing only on corporate event management. Things were going well until March 2020, when the pandemic hit. That year we were projected to do really well because we were growing at such a fast pace. Then everything just literally came to a halt. We are in the business of live events. So, when the government tells you, "You have to stay home", guess what happens to our business? It went to zero.

At the time it was very scary, and I was feeling very vulnerable because nothing was coming in for a while and I had a team to take care of. In that moment, despite the rampant uncertainties, I had a choice—to give up or to lean in and lead. I refused to take my foot off the pedal even though my back was against the wall. I knew I had to come out fighting like a warrior.

I have an awesome team that's like a family. So, my first thought was, "How do I take care of my team?" Physical safety was very important, so we sent the team to work from home before the government mandated us to. Next was, "OK, what do we do now?" Everybody is home, all the events were on hold or canceled, and we didn't know how long they would be on hold for. It was such a new thing, and it was very scary because of the stats that were being shown on the news. We had to adjust our mindset and figure out what was the solution that our client would want. What is their pain point now? Companies hire us because of connectivity and bringing their brands to live through event experiences.

We dive into those pain points. Brainstormed on many ideas on different offerings that will help close the gap on those pain points. Our team started researching virtual events and then did a lot of back-end work and testing to ensure we can deliver excellence even in virtual event experiences. Everyone at the company stepped up in different ways. We were all in it for the common goal. Then we were ready. We were one of the earlier adopters of virtual events. I'm here today, able to share that story, because of that. It was a lot of hard work and I just remember thinking to myself, "This ship is not going down on my watch." But in the beginning, there were moments where I just felt like I needed to cry. I even told my husband, "Maybe this is the year I will retire." Luckily, he didn't agree. So here I am still.

We offered virtual event management service and Events To Go Kits. Our mission is to help fuel brands to change lives for the better. For us, the event experience is all about making sure a well thought out attendee experience and fulfilling the KPI. We also love including surprise and delight moments. These Events To Go Kits could be shipped to the attendees' homes prior to the event to create some pre-event excitement or event FOMO. Then on the day of the virtual event, they can interact with the items that are in the box. That makes it so much more fun. Normally you are just receiving junk mail and bills to get a really delightful, curated box. Who doesn't love that? Our grit, persistence and resilience eventually paid off. We went from zero to more than 250 virtual events since March 2020. And the combination of the virtual event experiences and the Events To Go Kits were a big hit. Our mission really shined through, we were helping fuel brands to spark joy and bridge connectivity even during the pandemic. We are so grateful that not only did we survive the pandemic our business really thrived.

Q: That's so smart. My dad used to say, "The way you start a business is you find a need and fill it." So that's basically what you did. You sat down, thought about what the pain was, the need of the client, then you just filled that need. That's how you pivot and create magic. That's a real entrepreneur. Now you do both virtual and in-person events?

AM: Yes. We can do the whole mix now—live, virtual, or hybrid events. We already excelled at in person events previously, but now we have additional service offerings. If a company has an international team, we're able to add a virtual component so their international employees can participate as well.

Q: Amazing. What advice do you have for women looking to succeed in event management, as entrepreneurs, or just in the business world in general? What are some of the things that you could share from your own experience?

AM: I would advise women to work on their mindset. A lot of entrepreneurs don't take off because they are thinking, "Well, I don't have this," or "I can't do that." They're thinking about all the problems before they're thinking about what's possible.

Mindset is very important. You have to be able to take

that leap of faith, but calculated faith. You have to be able to cross over. It's funny you asked me that because I recently had a really close friend, a housewife, who wants to start a business because she has that opportunity. She's like, "I'm a mom. How do I do this?" I kind of walked her through it and she's like, "You know what? I can do it." I said, "Yes. Just keep telling yourself you can do it. And if you feel like you cannot, give me a call and I'll tell you you can!"

Another one is *excellence is a habit*. I have built an agency that is known to be excellent at what we do. We always try to find ways to add additional value for our clients. I believe exceeding expectations builds trust and creates customer loyalty. Wow Service is our standard. One of my favorite quotes is, "The difference between ordinary and extraordinary is that little extra." By Jimmy Johnson.

Q: I love that. What is inspiring you now? I used to ask the question "What motivates you?" But I think that a lot of entrepreneurs are self-motivated. So what is inspiring you?
AM: Two things. One is the community itself. I surround myself with other very successful entrepreneurs. They inspire me, they motivate me. The thing I learned is to not always be the smartest person in the room, because you can only go higher and get better, right? They'll help elevate you. Your network is your net worth.

Then two is making sure that you have a good support system within your own family, or your friends, your network—belonging to a community. I belong to group called Entrepreneurs' Organization where it's all entrepreneurs and we face a lot of the same problems. Find a network so that you have your version of a board of directors that you could go to for advice.

Q: That is awesome. What do you think, in general, tends to hold a lot of us back? A lot of women are like your friend who's a mom and decided, "OK, I want to do something." My sister actually just came to me. She's always been a manager and so she says, "I'm thinking about starting a business." What do you think we can do for other women to let them know that they can do it? What can we collectively share to let them know it's totally possible?

AM: Reading books like *Women Who BossUp* is very helpful! The more you read these stories, the more you say, "Hey, that could be me." But also, I think a big hindrance, at least based on my personal experience, is your mindset. I'd started out, like, "OK, let's slowly build this up." But now looking back, I held myself back because of that mentality.

I changed that mentality a few years ago to "I'm shooting for the moon and then I'll land among the stars." So much potential starts with the right mindset. Look at Elon Musk. He's always had huge visions and looks at where he ended up. Be bold, think bigger!

There are so many resources nowadays. Connect with other women entrepreneurs or talk to other business owners because they can help inspire you. If someone says no in terms of your idea, don't be shut down. Talk to a few more people. When I started my events agency, my first one, I actually interviewed someone in the industry and this particular gentleman told me, "Don't start this. It's so hard." But that lit a fire under me. I'm like, "I want to prove him wrong. I'm going to be more successful than he is."

Q: That is so very true. Women may be more qualified for something but the difference with men is they go into action. They just go. They'll already be at a seven-figure business and a woman is still at the starting gate going, "Should I do this? Do I have permission to do this?" I think that a lot of us hold ourselves back. Like you said, a lot of it has to do with mindset and not being willing to take the action and fail forward. Tell us about your clients. What kinds of corporations do you work with?

AM: We mainly focus on corporate and large community events. The three industries that we specialize in are tech, financial, and associations. Some of our clients are Google, TikTok, Facebook, East West Bank, CTBC Bank, and then lots of associations. We do work with others, like Toyota, but the three industries I mentioned are the three that we do most events for.

Q: Oh, my gosh, Amanda, this has been so much fun. Is there anything else you would like to share with my audience?

AM: I'll say two things. One is to make sure that you have your big-picture vision available. Your big-picture vision includes your mission and also your core values. Those elements lead all my actions and all my decisions, even when it comes to hiring. Our checklist for HR is going through that. Is this person a fit?

For example, one of our core values is "Wow Service." So, one of our interview questions is, "When was the last time you provided Wow Service?" It's very important that that is a very easy answer for that person. Also, we ask, "If on the client survey you receive a seven out of 10, what do you think?" People who pride themselves on Wow Service will say, "That's not good enough. I need a 10. Ten is what

I'm striving for." I had a candidate ask me one time, "What's wrong with seven?" I was like, "Nothing is wrong. We're just not a good fit." It has to come naturally.

Then also make sure you're thinking about a really, really strong company culture and then you're building in celebrations for your wins, whether big or small. Honestly, I used to not be good at that. I was good at celebrating the big wins, but I forget to celebrate the small wins. So, we started incorporating that into our weekly meetings and into our culture and it just makes it that much better. We do a company retreat every year. We also plan those for clients. Company retreats produce great results and ROI for the company because it allows your team to reconnect. When a company hosts frequent corporate events that bring everyone together, it provides the opportunity to network and get to know each other, encouraging more respect and emotional intelligence. Making the chain of communication stronger can only be a good thing!

As an Asian American woman in business during a time fraught with anti-Asian rhetoric and even violence toward members of my community, I wouldn't let those things stop me from succeeding.

Instead, I showed up more fully, more generously, and with gratitude for everything we have. It was important to me to model positive behavior for my kids, teaching them to be kind human beings who live a life of purpose—even in the face of what may seem like insurmountable challenges.

The result? We're still standing, and we're stronger than ever. At Innovate Marketing Group, we believe that our differences make us unique. We are proud to be a diverse, inclusive, 100% women-owned business. We believe that life is too short for boring events—and we continue to do what we do best and love what we do!

And during the last two years' VERY challenging times, we still manage to leverage our expertise and influence to help give back to the community.

Q: Yes. That's so good. How can people connect with you?
AM: People can find me at our website, innovatemkg.com. And I'm Amanda Ma on LinkedIn.

Q: Amanda, thank you so much. I'm so excited about all the stuff that we'll be doing together.
AM: Thank you so much.

AMANDA MA
www.innovatemkg.com

Amanda Ma is the Founder and CEO of Innovate Marketing Group, an award-winning experience agency based in Los Angeles that provides full-service event management service for top brands such as TikTok, Google, and East West Bank (Live, hybrid, virtual event experiences). Through her leadership, the company has flourished into one of the most distinguished experience agencies both locally and nationally.

Her mission is to help fuel brands to change lives for the better. Amanda has 17+ years of experience in business, event management & marketing. During the pandemic, her events company not only did not close but thrived. Her pandemic pivot story of 0 to 250 continues to shine to inspire others. She was named "Top 100 Most Influential People in the Event Industry Globally" by Eventex and Bizbash Top 500 most influential event professionals in the US. She is recognized as a business and community leader. She is also host of the EventUp Podcast. A collaborative leader, she is consistently sought out as a trusted strategic advisor. She currently sits on numerous boards. When she is not working with the White House or Secret Service, you can find her spending time with her family or traveling.

> You have to be willing to take that leap of faith, but calculated faith.
>
> —Amanda Ma

CRYSTAL D'CUNHA
The INSIDE View Inc.
Chief Experience Officer

CHAPTER 15

Creating Loyalty For Life
with Crystal D'Cunha

HEY THERE, BOSS LADIES. I AM SO EXCITED TODAY to have my next guest. We were just talking about the importance of leadership. I did some studying with John Maxwell and his leadership program and she also was trained through John Maxwell. Of course! So I'm excited to have this conversation because I think the world really needs a lot more leadership. Not only personal leadership, but leadership to guide people to the next level. She is the founder and chief experience officer of The INSIDE View, a leadership training and consulting company. She's also an award-winning customer experience engineer, sales training expert, executive leadership coach, and keynote speaker, and she is the driving force behind the world's number-one leadership training certification.

Q: Crystal D'Cunha, how are you?
Crystal D'Cunha: I'm wonderful, Tam. Thank you so much for having me. I'm so excited to chat with you.

Q: I'm excited to have you here. You're an award-winning entrepreneur, an international keynote speaker, a Customer Experience thought leader. What was your entrée into leadership, specifically?
CD: Great question. First of all, I'm so excited to join your community of great women leaders. My interest came from an early age. I'm the oldest of my family. I'm the first grandchild. And so I was literally born into a leadership role. But as I pursued my career, when I was about 16, I had a part-time job with a national retailer, and that is really where I developed my own leadership skills, as I learned from others.

They gave me opportunities outside of my hometown that were management and leadership roles. I was 19 when I started my first management position, and so it kind of happened by default and I quickly learned that leading a team was something that I just loved. People are often afraid of speaking in front of other people or making decisions. I was always the one to want to make decisions, and to be able to inspire and motivate. It was just something that came naturally.

Q: It makes sense that you're a number-one child. I'm number one as well. I'm not the number-one grandchild, I'm number two. But I totally get it, you're born into that role where your parents put you in charge. It was with three of us. I'm not sure how many siblings you had.
CD: There are three of us. Same thing.

Q: Yeah. And you're always the one. I became mommy junior or something, I think. And you just roll into that. I have always been intrigued by leadership and what it actually mean. Now that I've gotten older, I realize leadership doesn't just mean that you're leading a big pack. It could be a small pack. It could be leadership of yourself, right?
CD: Absolutely. It's a mindset. It's about self motivation, and being able to work on doubling down on your strengthens and learning how to embrace your challenges.

Q: What made you start your business? Going into leadership and being a leader at your job is one thing, but then going into companies to teach leadership is another.
CD: Absolutely. It was really by default, but has now happened by design. At the time, I was working as a Sales Manager for an Award Winning Home Builder and loved what I was doing. As I was leading their sales team and doing some exciting things, I felt that there was only so much I could do. And it was because I was not the boss. I was not the one really leading the whole picture. I was just leading a segment of what was happening.

I felt a bit like, if I can speak frankly, a caged animal. I just really wanted to run wild with my ideas to create dynamic Employee and Customer Experiences. I've been trained by Disney, I did work with the Tony Robbins team, and so I really filled my cup and I wanted to be able to lead and inspire others with all the knowledge I had, because I really felt that it would help others succeed. That is also where I saw a clear picture of what leadership looked like in 2015 compared to what I wanted leadership to look like. In that role I had to do a lot of the paperwork, I had to do a lot of the scheduling, stuff that I felt a junior person could do. If I was a leader, then my job was to be with my sales team, to be able to motivate them and inspire them constantly, to be listening and learning from our customers, not to be in the office dotting i's and crossing t's. That was where the disconnect is in many organizations. Senior level leaders hire great people, but that want to put them in a box, and limit them. If you put an Oak tree seed in a planter, it will only get as big as the planter. It will never get bigger than the environment it is in. That's how I felt, and that's how I was having to lead, my roots were breaking outside of the planter, if that makes sense?

So I started to define what leadership looked like for me, and I was to be able to lead people in a way that inspired people to grow as much or a little as they wanted. That is our job, to create environments where people can thrive and succeed. The administrative part in that role was supposed to be 80 percent of my role—as it is for most management roles! For most people in leadership roles, 60, 70, 80 percent of the role can boil down to an administrative task that can be coached and taught to somebody else. However, It's my belief that 80% of our work should be focused on creating an environment for our team and our people and our customers, right?

Q: **From an entrepreneurial standpoint, I can see that making a lot of sense. But I wonder if it's by design that a lot of companies don't want to have people going off on their own. I'm not sure. Because I felt the same way when I was in management, it was really a lot of administrative work and you were not encouraged to think on your own.**
CD: That's actually aligning really closely with what we're seeing right now in the labor market. The great resignation, the quiet quitters, we're hearing all about it. If you haven't created that environment—and even if you have, but are not maintaining it—you don't have a culture that can really hold onto people long term and through difficult times like we are seeing now.

You see, It's like a marriage. You've got to put the work in. I always say that if you treat your customers like prospects—and by customers, I mean both your employees and your paying customers—if you treat them like prospects, they'll never leave you. You have to speak the language of appreciation in the workplace, one that understands when to share words of affirmation, when to give quality time, when to serve, when to give a gift, and when a celebratory high five or a warm embrace is greatly needed.

Q: You just keep dating them and keep dating them, giving them wine, and bringing them flowers. Yeah, you're right.
CD: It's got to be genuine and you have to have a leadership mindset. I think one of the reasons I was successful in my retail career, where I had a training position, a management position, and spent almost 15 years, was that not only did I want to be successful, but it was so motivating and inspiring to me when they would send me somebody new or I would hire somebody with little experience and groom them, and

grow them, and then they'd go take on their multimillion-dollar store. It was just so rewarding.

That's what leadership looks like today—pushing people to succeed beyond ourselves. I've got a 19-year-old. All we want for our kids is to do better than us. That's all we want for our kids - right? And so why wouldn't we want that for the people that we're leading? We want to be able to push them beyond us, whether it's within our own work environment or another work environment. We really have to have that mindset and that genuine care to see others succeed.

Q: That's very true. How do you run your leadership program for companies?
CD: Well, I'll pat ourselves on the back, we just won an International Stevie Award for our Leadership Experience Excellence (LXE) training certification program, beating out IBM and a few other bigwigs. It's an eight-week program with long term follow up, and it is designed for leadership teams to take together. We won't accept just one person from the leadership team, it's typically the entire decision-making team and then some. We really like to invite those inspiring to be leaders in the organization into the training as well. We start off with vision vitals and we get into lovesick leadership, culture connection, trusting top talent, designing your environment to delight, how to coach and inspire, and, of course, sales and marketing.

So we focus on those every week for eight weeks. After that, we create a 12-week plan where they'll be able to accomplish goals every 12 weeks. Then we follow up with them consistently to make sure that the needle is moving forward. And sometimes it doesn't move forward. It's not a magic wand. So it'll give you the principles and the structures you need in today's leadership world, what leadership looks like in 2022. Because it's different today than it was five years ago, even though it was two years ago.

We've put intuitive and tangible tools within the program tools that can be actioned and used right away!. We talk about diversity, equity, and inclusion. If you're trying to grow your business, are you connecting with diverse markets? We also spend a lot of time on employee experience. If you're trying to grow your team, are you advertising and attracting only a specific market? Or are you opening up your doors to all people?

I'll share a quick story with you. I just got a call from a potential client who said, "Crystal, we need some help hiring great talent and cultivating a good experience for our employees." They want to hire new people. So I booked a meeting with them. Then the other day I was driving down the road and I saw a billboard that they had posted. The billboard said, "We're hiring," and it had at least 30 people on there. And all of the 30 people…

Q: …are Caucasian. I notice it every time.
CD: You notice it every time, I notice it every time, and any person of color notices it every time. I hope our allies out there notice it as well. But I thought, well, of course you're having a hard time attracting people, you've narrowed your own market. Of course. I'm having a conversation with them next week, but I thought: Here's the problem. You know, you had 30 people. You should have just said, "We're hiring," and not put a picture up. You would've been better off. So now you've just detracted, literally, in our region, I don't know, 75 percent of people. We're becoming more and more diverse daily. But it's not just people of color, it's

also allies and the younger generation. They will not work for an organization that's not inclusive, and they're recognizing that. AND… The customers wanting to do business with them…they have just narrowed that market as well, because as a woman of color, they all not be my first choice simply because of my perception of the organization.

Q: It's very true. They have to get with it. What is the most difficult thing you've experienced as a woman in business or in your personal life? What are some challenges that you have encountered?
CD: I'll give you two. I'll start off with personal and then I'll dive into professional. So personally, you know, as an independent mom, my son, like I said, is 19 now, and I'm thrilled at the journey he's taken, the habits he's embraced, and he is off to university. But as an independent parent, there's nowhere to go. There's no crutch to lean on. Succeed or fail, it was all on me. I always thought to myself, what I'm currently making is equal to what I'm currently doing.

And so that mindset was also challenging because I didn't want to sleep. Because I thought, OK, if I work a little harder, I'll be able to earn a little more. If I do a little more, I'll make a little more, right? And so in one way, that was great, but it was very difficult and it still is. We've got a home, we live a full family lifestyle now, but we saw the bottom of the barrel. And it was definitely a tricky time. There were times where lights were cut off and cars were repossessed and notices were given. We lived through those days. And it's just a joy and a blessing to see what life's like now, but really, succeed or fail, it's all on you. It's challenging to keep your mind focused on our WHY when God throws you a curveball. But Faith and fear can't live in the same heart, so everyday, You have to choose, and choosing FAITH is my default!

Q: We were talking about that briefly, and I've experienced that. That's real. It's scary.
CD: I get choked up thinking about it. Those days were tough. But Life happens for us, not to us!

From a professional point of view, one of the bigger challenges was the industry that I'm in. I work with every industry in terms of type of business, but what I'm teaching, the skillset is leadership. And again, understanding diversity here, I'm a woman and I'm a woman of color. According to the diversity chart, that's kind of the bottom of the barrel right?

So trying to go into established businesses who are really wanting to make a shift in employee experience and customer experience and be open to diversity, equity, and inclusion, here's me coming into a business that's most likely owned and operated by Caucasian men or Caucasian people in general—that was tricky. Because how are they going to trust me? And sometimes unconsciously, sometimes consciously. It's not intentional always, sometimes it's just we do business with people like us, people we like and trust. I really had to learn how to develop trust. And I've done it. I've done it well now, but in the beginning it was tricky. For me, when I'm establishing trust, it's really about trying to teach somebody something new. If I'm able to teach them something new, and I hear, "Tell me more about that, Crystal," then I've got trust; I value that so much, and it's mine to lose.

Q: Yes. That's so good. I was thinking about your experience as a woman of color going to companies who want a new experience, they want to give people a diverse experience of their company. You would seem to me to be the best person to bring them on board, because you have had all the experiences of a person of color, right? You can come in and you can relate and you can create programming that can be relatable. I would see that as a definite asset to work with you as a company.

CD: In the last two years in particular, I am using that as a strength and it is coming across, but that's simply because the world has changed over the last few years. So there's an intentionality behind a lot of that, and I appreciate it. It's working. But it wasn't always that way.

Q: It wasn't always that way. What is inspiring you now? I used to ask people what is motivating them, but I find that a lot of entrepreneurs are self-motivated, but they're inspired every day by something, to get up and go forward and move and work hard and create and all these things.

CD: Something comes to mind right away when you ask me that. I'm thinking of a phone call I had this weekend, on Saturday. I was driving home from Toronto and one of my clients texted me in a frantic panic. You know, I don't want to bug you on a weekend, da, da, da, da, da. And they had a challenge going on and I picked up the phone and I called her and she said, "Oh, my gosh, you're calling me on a weekend?" I said, "Of course. Talk to me, what's going on?" And I had an hour-and-a-half drive from Toronto back to Niagara and we talked the whole way, I listened, learned, coached her through everything, we worked out a plan.

That's inspiring. Well over 90 percent of businesses now

are small businesses. And for small businesses to be able to make a change in their structures, in their processes, but most important, in their finances, being able to be financially strong because of advice that I give them or guidance I give them or training I've given them, it's pretty exciting to me. Larger organizations come to me often and I will consult or train larger organizations but I really like to work with the small business. They're agile, there's no red tape, and we can test something and if it works, it works, it's great, and it can transform them from a $100,000 business to a $1 million business to a $10 million business in record time, just because of some process structures and changes we do. One organization we worked with went from four employees to 14 employees in two years, just because of the way we design things. And when you go from 4 to 14, your revenue model changes as well. And so when business owners are able to be open-minded and see the big picture, they can often see it and they've maybe even seen it before I got there, but because we're entrepreneurs, there's nobody holding us accountable. And so when I'm able to hold them accountable and ask, "Why not? Why haven't we moved that forward?" That's starting to really change.

Q: I love that. What would you tell a business owner who is trying to develop programs and grow their business in this climate? What are the most important things to focus on first?

CD: Their employees. Their employee experience. 110 percent. It is the biggest missing factor, because when business owners typically start businesses—or even, you know, we've worked with businesses that are 20, 40 years old and it's worked. "It's not broken, Crystal, we don't need to fix it, everything's working." And by that they mean bills are getting paid.

But in this day and age, you're getting compared based on the experience that you deliver. From an employee's perspective, people don't want to work with businesses that aren't innovative and moving forward. And so, really designing an experience that delights is critical, and we teach you that in Leadership Experience Excellence.

You have two customers: your internal customer and your external customer. Your internal customer, of course, is your employees, but also, it's your partners in business, your trades that you might work with, your banker, your accountant, all the people that help your business run, they're all your internal customers. They have to be raving fans, they have to find value in you and just love doing business with you. That's when they can transfer those emotions to your customer. If you want to create loyalty for life, it's really focusing on that employee experience. It's not about paying people more. It's about designing something that works for them, and truly appreciating them as an individual - Hey it's a human need to feel significant, be intentional about making people feel significant.

Q: I love that. Crystal, this is so good. Is there anything else that you would like to share with my audience? We want to tell them exactly where they can find you, how they can learn about your business, how they can connect with you on social media, but is there anything else you'd like to share first?

CD: Yes. Often small businesses will say, "Well, Crystal, we're not like Disney. We can't do it the way Disney does it or Google does it.". To those small businesses, I'll leave you with this: It's not about having a big budget. It's just about taking action and really designing something that works best for both the employees and the customers. It's really thinking about those things. Some of the tools that we use are employee journey mapping and customer journey mapping, which means being able to identify the emotional experience that somebody is having, the journey they are going on when they visit your website, when they go on your Facebook page, wherever they're going to find you. The way they feel when someone picks up the phone, or doesn't pick up the phone?

Often companies just focus on one channel to bring a really good experience to people. But I want them to think about all the channels that customers and employees come into. Are they receiving the same experience on every channel? The same high-quality, white-glove service that you probably have in your mission statement. Am I receiving that kind of quality service from every channel? Because you can't just select one area. I'll hear, "Oh, our website is perfect and they come in through our website." Well, there are 10 steps before your website, and 89 percent of people, if they don't like doing business with you on their preferred channel, won't come back. So that's what I would encourage business owners to do. Really look at all your channels and design them to delight - then test them again and again.

Q: That includes clients as well as vendors?
CD: It does. Part of our methodology is to ignite leaders, excite employees, and then together, delight your customers. When I say ignite leaders, it's not just the people around your boardroom table, it's the leaders that are helping you build your product or service. All the vendors, all

the people involved in allowing you to do the business that you're doing, right? They need to be ignited and inspired with a really clear mission and a really clear vision. But not just words on a website. How do you live that vision and mission? How do you practice that vision and mission every single day? What are the tangible things you need to do to live out missions and visions? Those are the tools we need to give our leaders. This is what needs to happen every day to live this out. Because there's such a gray area between a vision statement or a mission statement, and actually practicing it. What does it mean? What does "good service" mean? We need those tangibles.

Q: We absolutely do. Let's share how people can connect with you.
CD: The website is gettheinsideview.com and I'm pretty much all over social media. On Instagram I'm @crystld and @gettheinsidevu. You can also find me on Facebook and LinkedIn. I love connecting with people, so please feel free to reach out with questions and I'm happy to help. In particular, If you a a business leader who is feeling stuck, and are ready to start working ON your business and not IN your business, If you are ready to be known and well respected for cultivating a culture of success, being a coveted place to work, building loyalty for life, having a 5 start service legacy, and consistently deliver delight and providing exceptional customer experiences - then don't hesitate to connect!

Q: Awesome, Crystal, thank you. I'm looking forward to all the stuff that we'll be doing this year.
CD: My pleasure! Thank you for having me and I look forward to it.

CRYSTAL D'CUNHA

gettheinsideview.com

Crystal D'Cunha is the driving force behind the World's #1 Leadership Training Certification; Customer Experience Mastery!

Crystal is an award-winning entrepreneur, international keynote speaker, and CX thought leader who has spent nearly two decades in the corporate world directing, coaching and leading sales forces valued at more than $100 million. She is the charismatic force behind the world's #1 Leadership training program, Customer Experience Mastery. Her certification through the Disney Institute, Tony Robbins, and the John Maxwell Institute and her real-world experience has led her to her current role as President and CEO of The INSIDE View, Inc.; a Customer Experience Design Firm, Specializing in Design thinking, Leadership training, Employee engagement and Diversity, Equity and Inclusion. In addition to her passion for Customer Experience Design, Crystal contributes to her community as a founding member of Women in CX, A Director on the CXPA Toronto Board, is the Chair of GroYourBiz Niagara, and is the President of the Ad & Sales Association.

Crystal's methodology of Igniting Leaders, Exciting Employees and Delighting Customers has allowed her to help organizations across the globe see outstanding results in employee engagement, productivity, and customer satisfaction!

Inspiration came to me as an understanding of what starts to move when we are in our hearts sincerely to care.

—Crystal D'Cunha

> If you want things to change, get comfortable being uncomfortable.
>
> —Tam Luc

GAIL MERIEL
Success Redefined
Motivational Speaker, Founder of Success Redefined

CHAPTER 16

Reassess Your Definition of Success
with Gail Meriel

HEY THERE, SUPERWOMEN. I AM SO EXCITED today to have my next guest. She hails from one of my favorite cities in the U.S., Chicago. And she's pretty much going through the process of building her business very similar to the way I did. She is working a full-time job, building her consulting firm, working with people and learning and growing. It's really exciting. And I love when I meet people who are at this stage in their business, especially with the background that she has. She went through a lot of self-discovery, successes, and failures, so she is bringing a lot to the table to help people. She also has 25 years of career experience in Corporate America.

Q: Gail Meriel, how are you?
Gail Meriel: Good, Tam. I'm so happy to be here. Thank you for having me.

Q: I'm excited to have you here. I was reading about your business and about how you had gone through what a lot of people actually go through, which is imposter syndrome and really holding themselves back. Sometimes it's based on how they were raised or negativity they've faced in their careers or in their lives, whatever makes them think "I'm not good enough for this" or "I'm not smart enough" or "I don't have enough degrees." And when you started sharing your experiences with that, you found that it was really helpful for other people.
GM: Yes, absolutely. According to the American Psychological Association, about 82 percent of us experience imposter syndrome, and 65 percent of us are professionals. As I went through my challenges in the corporate landscape, as well as my successes, there were some things that really impacted me. And as women, we tend to internalize everything. Is it really me? What could I have done differently? Am I way in over my head? That kind of thing. That's the mentality that I had for a while. And it was so depressing that I ended up having to really reassess myself as a professional. I was hoping that I could be of more service to folks and be able to really coach them through their challenges as I went through mine. In fact, I would love to tell you the story of my aha moment and the breakthrough that I went through.

Q: I want to hear it! Before we go there, let's spend another minute on imposter syndrome because I really am curious about whether this is something that shows up for women more than men. Or does it seem to affect all genders equally?

GM: I believe it affects all of us equally, but I believe women deal with it differently. Women internalize it, whereas, in my experience, men brush it off and they're able to get back in the game. When women internalize it, we try not to let it affect us, but because we're both more in touch with our emotions and harder on ourselves, it tends to affect us more. I've done research and I've seen some celebrities—a lot of them men, even including Tom Hanks—who are affected by imposter syndrome because of certain failures or maybe some negative feedback they received that really affected them, that resulted in the tendency toward imposter syndrome.

Q: Got you. OK, so what changed all that for you? What was the aha moment?

GM: I went through a period of time where I was really assessing my career based on a situation that I ran into. I'm an IT project manager and one of the credentials in my industry—actually, it's the mother of all certifications, the Project Management Professional certification, or PMP—is one that every project manager strives to get in order to be credible in that industry, in that profession. Earning the PMP means more opportunities and better opportunities. I was a project manager for many years and a lot of my mentors and colleagues began to say, "This is a great time for you to get certified."

So I did a lot of intense studying, I had a mentor who

actually guided me on how to study. A lot of colleagues and friends that I knew had a self-study method. There was a point A to point B way of going through the process. In any professional or standard exam, there are tips, strategies, secrets to success, that kind of thing. So when I thought I was ready, I went into the exam all positive, all optimistic, and then I failed it. And it was like, "Okay, I was a project manager for so many years. Why couldn't I do this?" I knew the questions, I had passed so many practice exams, what happened? So my mentor and I went through it and decided to just focus on the areas where I did poorly and then I'd get the confidence to be able to pass the second time around.

So I went through that again. I did intense studying while working full time and trying to keep a family together, managing the household. And this time I felt more confident. I said, "Okay, I'm going to get this. I'm going to do this again." Second time, I failed once more. At this point, I lost all my motivation. I was so deflated and I was really internalizing everything, and saying, "OK, it's really me this time." A lot of colleagues of mine passed on the first try.

So I ended up taking a break from it, taking a few months away, because I was really mentally drained, emotionally drained. I had challenges at work and I wanted to really focus on my career and get my projects off the ground. But when the one-year mark of starting this journey came about, I really was assessing it. And I said, okay, I really want to finish what I started. I know I'm a great professional, I know I'm smart. I'm a lifelong learner, Tam.

Q: I know! Don't you have an MBA too?

GM: Yes. So I reassessed everything from my learning style to my mental capacity to my learning environment. And I just really tried to break it down and turn it around into a positive experience. So I ended up taking a bootcamp class to study for the exam. And it was very helpful for me because I learn by learning from others and by doing. And so just that interaction with others and having them explain to me what I did wrong and being interactive with them as to what my logic was versus what was actually the correct answer, I was able to get that secret sauce. The aha moment of saying, "Okay, that's why that response was wrong." And it boosted my confidence a lot more because I was able to get that interaction.

And they were actually great cheerleaders. The instructor was a really great cheerleader for me as well. As I did the practice exams, I knew exactly what was going on. So after a yearlong journey, I took the exam for the third and last time. And this time it was really interesting because I finished the exam pretty early. Whereas the first two times, I ran out of time because I had so much anxiety. Then I changed my strategy a bit. Instead of going back and reviewing my answers, I stayed where I was. Because I knew that I was second-guessing myself and then changing the answers. My mentor had told me, "Do not change your answers because usually your gut feeling is the right one."

So I finished the exam early and I clicked on the submit button and I finally was able to pass the exam. Later on, I found out that I exceeded the passing score. So it was just that moment where—when I saw the results, I was still on camera because it was a virtual exam, I just screamed up in the air. I didn't care if the proctor online was still seeing me. And my tears were flowing and I just totally screamed. Because all the months of anxiety, imposter syndrome, second-guessing myself all the time, and just the frustration and the mental burnout was released.

Q: What do you think happened differently the third time? When you think about the whole thing?
GM: I did some tactical thinking and I made some tactical changes, like going through the boot-camp class, doing a one-on-one interaction versus trying to study on my own. A lot of people do learn on their own and they are successful, but I had to dig deep inside and soul search. So I was able to go through that interaction with a group class. But for me, it was more confidence.

It was more about what I think I could do and what I can control versus what I couldn't control, especially how tough the exam was, but I could control how I react to it. At the same time, I redefined what success really meant to me. Did I really want those three letters behind my name to be credible as a professional? Or did I also want to resonate with the content and what the exam questions were asking me and to really be seen as an expert? When that really dawned on me, I realized that I had the control to be able to look at that with a different perspective.

Q: That is incredible. A couple things I learned from this conversation: Don't quit. Just don't quit. And so that's the first part of this lesson, you did not quit. You got back in there, you dusted yourself off, you did it a different way. Ultimately, I think you knew you were good enough. And the second thing is you learned to believe in yourself.
GM: Yes, yes. That's the key. There are a few things that

I did to take care of myself as well, and some strategies that helped me along the way to get that confidence. Like practicing self-care and connecting with others so they can give you a different perspective. Even if it's not on that topic, just being around people and connecting with others helps me put things into perspective so I can be reminded that there is an optimistic view of challenges. And then also developing healthy coping skills, having a tactical way of addressing the issue rather than just letting it weigh me down. That really improved my emotional intelligence and being able to move on from that challenge.

Q: I love this story. What would you tell another woman who is experiencing a lack of confidence? She's trying to do some big things in her life. What would you tell her to do? Reassess your goals, really assess your definition of success. And as I mentioned earlier, redefine your success. If you feel that there's something that's not right, and that you're not successful in what you're looking to do, really redefine that. What are your goals? What are your short-term and long-term goals and where do you see yourself? There are different ways to be successful.

I've tried to chase titles, but when I look at myself and I say, "OK, why do you want to chase titles? Do you want the leadership role? Do you want to make an impact on others?" That's where I really was able to get that aha moment, because I do want to be a leader. And speaking out my story, as well as coaching other women, are things that help me in being a leader. To me, that's more success than any title. I feel that you can be a leader no matter how you position yourself. My advice is to really reassess and redefine what success means to you.

Q: So good. Is there anything else you can share about your journey building a business? Being in Corporate America is quite a bit different than entrepreneurship. You're bringing a lot of your knowledge and experience into entrepreneurship, but there is also a new skill set. Because it's all on you. You have to get the clients, you have to figure out the offer, all these things.
GM: It is a very eye-opening experience. It's a slow experience for me and I am leaning on awesome coaches to help me through. I'm an avid reader, and I'm reading a book called *The E-Myth Revisited* By Michael Gerber.

Q: Yes, I've heard that's a great book.
GM: I'm learning from that, as well as leaning into the coaches that are helping me and guiding me through the process of defining how I want my business model to be. I really love speaking, I really love helping others. And when I help others, I see their light bulb goes on as well. I've been told that I'm the type of person who people go to just to talk through things. I have that personality that people are comfortable with. And that's what really helps me be able to help others as well and be successful at it.

Q: What is inspiring you right now? What is motivating you on this journey?
GM: What's inspiring me is what I went through and how I can help others. As I mentioned earlier, I do consulting with colleagues or with friends and they see the benefit. I know I have a gift and I want to share that with the world. That's what's inspiring me. I've gone through a lot of negative situations, that I know a lot of people have gone through or are going through. And if I can impact

someone, even just one person, I've reached my goal. So that's really what inspires me, is to share what I know to the world so everybody else can be successful.

Q: Gail, this is so fun. I'm glad that we are working on this new project together. Where can people find you? And what is your niche audience?

GM: I'm looking to expand, but right now I am really focusing on women in corporate who are experiencing imposter syndrome because of their situations. I can be reached at my website, www.gailmeriel.com, and I can be reached through LinkedIn and Clubhouse.

Q: Having the skill of project management is really helpful for a coach. It would really help somebody who has imposter syndrome. Someone's going through something, they want to get something done, they don't think they're good enough, but they want next steps. You know what you're doing, you've been doing this a long time. I think it would be great to connect with you, Gail, thank you so much.

GM: Thank you, Tam. Talk to you soon. Talk to everyone soon.

GAIL MERIEL
www.gailmeriel.com

Gail Meriel is a Project Manager, Award-winning Motivational Speaker, Author and Mindset Coach. She is a Sr. Consultant with Unify Consulting, LLC and is the Founder of Success Redefined. She has an MBA degree and PMP certification, plus has over 25 years of experience with working for Fortune 500 companies.

Gail is a Co-Author of Inspiring Women Professionals Who Boss Up. Gail helps inspire and empower women who lost confidence or feel unworthy from failure and self-doubt learn how to regain self-esteem through self-discovery and overcome imposter syndrome so they can take controllable action, to redefine their success and become Warriors with a Purpose. Visit www.gailmeriel.com to learn more.

Reassess and redefine what success means to you. If you feel that there's something that's not right in what you're looking to do, really redefine that.

—*Gail Meriel*

SECTION 4

What's Next

TAM R. LUC
Delucslife Media, Women who BossUp,
Women with Vision International, CEO/ Founder

Stepping into the shoes of an entrepreneur
with Tam Luc

I'VE NOTICED THAT SOME PEOPLE HAVE A HARD time taking on the title of entrepreneur. Even if, by definition, that's what they are.

Is it too big a word?

Let's explore some definitions.

First let's take the word *business*. To be in business is to be in the practice of making a living by engaging in commerce. You're marketing and selling to make a profit. A business begins with an idea for connecting clients with what they need and want.

But when can you call yourself an entrepreneur? Do you have to wait until you start making a profit?

An entrepreneur is an individual who creates a new business, bearing most of the risks and enjoying most of the rewards from that business. Entrepreneurs are innovators, sources of new ideas, goods, or services, creators of new business categories or programs.

The formal definition of *entrepreneurship* is the creation of a new business that aggregates capital and labor in order to produce goods or services for profit. But in my view, you are an entrepreneur as soon as you come up with a new business idea.

Because entrepreneurship is usually not taught in schools, it's foreign to many of us. However, being an entrepreneur is the same as being a leader or innovator. Being a leader requires making the choice to completely overhaul our behaviors. With practice, these behaviors become habits. With time, these habits lead to our success.

I wonder if the gravity of what is possible prevents some of us from owning who we are.

When I was developing a book called *Visionary Women who BossUp*, I had the hardest time filling the book with authors because so many women were afraid to own that title. Many of the women we interviewed were not ready to be called visionaries. I found it so interesting.

Some women also have expressed to me that "BossUp" is a heavy word they do not feel worthy of. I personally define BossUp as believing in yourself. But maybe it feels bigger than that to some. Anyway, back to the point.

Could this be another example of our own self-imposed limitations? Do definitions or identities require approval by others? Can I call myself an entrepreneur if all I have is an idea of what I'm going to sell? Am I a visionary if I'm the only one setting that vision at the moment? Or can I BossUp anytime I want?

When do I get to slide into those big girl shoes? Maybe we

already have those shoes on our feet but we need to realize our own greatness.

What do you think?

TAM LUC
www.delucslife.com

After years of struggling in business and experiencing the ups and downs of life. Tam speaks on what finally turned her life around and how she created a multi-six figure business in less than 2 years. She shares her secrets on how anyone can use their own story to nail their core message and create a huge impact in the world.

Number one bestselling author of *A Women's Side Hustle* and the *Women Who BossUp* book series, International Speaker with 22 years of entrepreneurial and investment experience now giving her heart to doing what she loves for women that are working hard to find their way.

LET'S BE social

@womenwithvisioninternational

Do you have a BossUp moment in your life?
We want to hear your story.

Email us at: support@delucslife.com